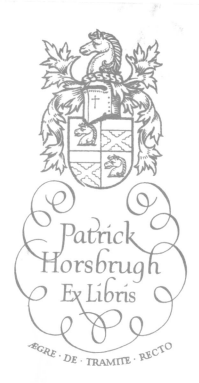

Steam Horse: Iron Road

STEAM HORSE: IRON ROAD

Edited by Brenda Horsfield

British Broadcasting Corporation

The photograph on the preceding pages
shows the train sheds at King's Cross
in the days of steam

© The Contributors and
the British Broadcasting Corporation 1972

First published 1972
ISBN 0 563 10692 1

Published by the British Broadcasting Corporation
35 Marylebone High Street, London W1M 4AA

Printed in England by Jolly and Barber Ltd, Rugby

Contents

LANDMARKS IN RAILWAY HISTORY

1802 Richard Trevithick's first locomotive tested
at Coalbrookdale ironworks

1804 Trevithick's Pen-y-Darran locomotive tested

1808 Trevithick's last locomotive *Catch me who Can* runs in London

1813 First commercially successful locomotives built for Middleton
Colliery Railway to designs of Matthew Murray and John Blenkinsop

Puffing Billy built by William Hedley for Wylam Colliery

1814 George Stephenson builds his first locomotive, the *Blücher*

1825 Stockton and Darlington Railway opens

1829 Rainhill Trials won by Stephenson's *Rocket*

Stourbridge Lion, first locomotive in the United States,
imported from England

1830 Liverpool and Manchester Railway opens

1833 First of Robert Stephenson's 'Patentee' locomotives built

1835 German Railways inaugurated with *Der Adler*

1839 Opening of Robert Stephenson's London to Birmingham line

1841 Completion of the London to Bristol line of
Isambard Kingdom Brunel's Great Western Railway

1849 Disgrace of George Hudson 'the Railway King'

1883 First electric railway in Britain opened at Brighton by Magnus Volk

1923 'Grouping' of over 100 independent railway companies into larger units

1926 *Mallard* establishes world speed record for steam at 126 mph

1948 Nationalisation of independent companies into British Railways.

1968 Last steam locomotives run regular services on British main lines

Introduction

BRENDA HORSFIELD

Little girls are not usually encouraged to want to be engine drivers, even today when the job could plausibly be described as a nice, clean, sedentary occupation for a steady type of woman. Before diesels and electrics finally took over on British railways an 'engine' was usually a splendid and impressive steam locomotive, a magnificent monster towering over the track, and an engine driver in his cab cut a figure as commanding as a king. But as a child I was only one generation removed from a family business of locomotive building and my parents took it for granted that any normal person would want to drive engines, and indeed, any other kind of moving machinery. They solemnly laid out a 15″ gauge model railway round our few acres of garden, rough pasture and woodland, so that the track made a circle a quarter of a mile in circumference. On this, for a few glorious years, we took it in turn to drive a succession of gorgeous and exotic ¼ scale steam locomotives, followed by a 'train' of two open carriages that could carry something like twenty passengers at a time. We puffed up an inclined embankment, over a bridged stream, through a satisfactorily deep cutting and even a tunnel, before swooping downhill again and reversing into the station.

The needs of locomotives for water and good quality steam coal, their performance on incline or curve, were as familiar to us as the steering characteristics of the family car and it seemed no more eccentric to put a spirit level over the line after a rainy spell than to take the dog for a walk. With our chatter about fishplates, dogspikes, ballast, whistles, signals and brakes, I suppose that to outsiders we must have presented all the symptoms of incipient dottiness. But when, like all good things, it came to an end, it had at least one long-term result that no one could have foreseen. Fifteen years after our last train ran home and our rails were grubbed up and carried off by other enthusiasts, I found myself undertaking, without a moment's hesitation, the task of producing a BBC television series about the history of steam railways. And it is to that series, *Steam Horse : Iron Road*, that this book owes both its existence and its name.

Just what should go into the series was a matter for lengthier consideration and a lot of debate between myself, the production team and our various advisers. The choice of material, and even of approach to it, was enormous. Even the most superficial reading of nineteenth-century history makes it clear that the story of railways, of their slow beginning and their later explosive growth, is totally entangled with the story of the development of British industry and British society. Any treatment that attempts to isolate the railway story from its proper background will be both unscholarly and misleading. For special conditions created the railways. Pre-industrial Britain had a system of freehold land tenure, a thrusting and ambitious middle class and an army of available landless labourers that made it a society uniquely prepared to inaugurate a new age. However much the railways appear to have sprung from individual genius and seized opportunities, they came to meet an urgent commercial need for faster and cheaper transport than the under-developed roads or the exorbitantly-priced canals could provide. Yet even if the first railways were conjured up for the profit of the few front-runners of an economy that moved at the pace of the horse, the consequences, in a single decade, condemned a whole society to be swept away and almost at a stroke created the modern world.

The speed and cheapness of railways for the movement of goods and people immediately gave to their users an advantage so powerful that no one could resist their competition and survive. So railways inevitably bred more railways, and gave a fantastic acceleration to the rate of industrial growth. The demand for iron rails alone, in the boom years of 1845-50, ran at $1\frac{1}{2}$ million tons a year and called into existence the production capacity that was to become the steel industry. Railways made towns out of villages and hamlets, they scattered the workers of the towns into dormitory suburbs along their lines, they created both the need and the means for an immense holiday industry, they required and created systems of operation, time-keeping and communication that shape the pattern of our lives today. And in doing all this they rushed us headlong and unprepared towards today's problems – the huge urban labour forces that fall a helpless prey to the slightest recession; the devouring industrial development of the countryside; the exploitation and pollution; the increasing demand for power and fuel and mineral resources; the competitive pressures for personal mobility that are putting every family, possibly every individual, into a motor car; the tourist tide that is covering every picturesque shoreline in the world with holiday hotels and villas.

The background, then, is as important as the foreground in the railway scene but for the purposes of television too much scene-setting can obscure the pattern of the main story; it is only too easy to hide the wood with trees, branches, leaves and even undergrowth. But in any case, by the time I started my deliberations, television had already taken several bites at railway history. Dramas, documentaries and various magazine programmes had dealt with the amazing work of the navvies, with the building of the Woodhead tunnel, with the passing of the age of steam, the coming of the sensational new electric lines of the future, and the efforts of railway preservation societies in saving individual lines. Indeed there had been an entire 'educational' series devoted to the social history of the railway age, an impressive body of work even though it had only been seen by viewers in the Manchester area.

My series, however, had the new advantage of colour through which even familiar visual material would be rejuvenated. Even the loyal market for railway books is not large enough for all their illustrations to be in colour and pictures that turn up time and again as black-and-white photographic reproductions often conceal the fact that their originals were wonderfully evocative paintings. Apart from this, what would be most interesting to see at this moment in time, it seemed to me, was the *hardware* of the railways – the tangible, visible, often gorgeously decorated remains of the locomotives, carriages, and stations, and the achievements of civil engineering, all of which are to some extent threatened by the ravages of time and change. This series would therefore lean heavily in the direction of historic railway technology.

Even after the decision had been made to start squarely with the locomotive it was not entirely simple to begin. The build-up to the first locomotive, indisputably the brain-child of Richard Trevithick, reaches backwards in time not just into the eighteenth century but into the declining years of the seventeenth as well. It goes back through the rise of the Cornish engines to the 'patents' they were built to outwit on James Watt's engines and the crippling 'share of savings' he charged for their use. Then back further still to the 'atmospheric' engines put together in the early 1700s by a nonconformist Dartmouth blacksmith, Thomas Newcomen, who, ahead of all the scholarly 'scientists' of the day, solved the problem that had been holding up the whole advance of Western European industrialisation. This was the need to find a power unit to drive pumps that could drain the mines, descending ever deeper below the water-table in search of essential metals and coal. The needs of these 'pre-industrial' mines of the sixteenth and seventeenth centuries were leading to the production of the locomotive – the 'steam horse'. They were also starting the trail that led to the 'iron road' with the trackway, or 'tram' of wooden rails (not yet made of expensive iron), that by lowering friction on wagon wheels, reduced the effort of miners moving heavy loads of ore along the galleries.

The true historian and the industrial archaeologist will want to examine every step of the way to the locomotive with loving attention. To the casual television viewer, perhaps even the railway enthusiast, the arrival on the scene of the machine itself would surely be going back quite far enough. The changes between Trevithick's first experimental design and the triumphant success of the Stephensons' *Rocket* at the Rainhill Trials of 1829 promised an introductory programme that would effectively herald the birth of the modern railway system when the Liverpool and Manchester Railway opened on 15 September, 1830.

The relics of this historic period are now priceless national treasures and a substantial proportion of what exists is preserved in the Science Museum at South Kensington, London. Surprisingly, in view of the nostalgia for old steam railways in recent years, some of the great showpieces – the original *Puffing Billy*, *Sans Pareil* and *Rocket* – have not previously been shown on television. The museum staff who spend their time caring for them and who polished an extra sparkle into them for our cameras were delighted that their charges were at last receiving their proper tribute of admiration.

As well as these precious early locomotives the Science Museum also preserves many minor relics of the early railways, a superb collection of models and a number of significant paintings. In the event, to open the series we moved ourselves into the Museum with electronic cameras, using the railway collection as our studio and John van Riemsdijk as our knowledgeable and sympathetic guide to the exhibits. For movement we used archive film and reconstructions, shot on the occasion of various railway centenary celebrations including the Stockton and Darlington Centenary in 1925 and the German Railway Centenary in 1935.

From this temporary base in the Science Museum we also started our later programme 'Locomotives in Action', the account, essential to the series, of how the ancestral *Rocket* design and its variations developed into the later great giants of steam, and how eventually these famous locomotives gave way, under certain circumstances of economic pressure and traffic density in the technically advanced countries, to the diesel and electric locomotives of today and tomorrow.

Any television programme on a historical subject is likely to rely heavily on library and archive film of past or distant events. This programme, however, brought me an unexpected opportunity of adding a contribution to that 'archive' store. While it was being prepared British Rail decided to relent from its declared policy of no more steam over its metals to allow *King George V* and a train of pullman carriages (all now entrusted to the care of the Bulmers Cider Company) to run from Olympia to Swindon, to see whether occasional steam excursions for the benefit of enthusiasts were a practical possibility.

Filming such a run successfully is an expensive operation. Any cameraman on the ground, beside the track, gets one shot as the train rushes past him. For full coverage several men would be needed. A cameraman on board the train can only get pictures of the carriage interiors, and of the view from the windows – another man would be needed for the cab, and so on. Single documentary programmes like the famous treatment of the anniversary run of *The Flying Scotsman* may involve a dozen or more separate camera crews. Fortunately, for my purposes both the BBC London and South West news programmes were interested in the run of *King George V* and by sharing costs with them it was possible to cover the run from all points of view. My contribution was to direct the filming of shots from a helicopter, preferably over the stretch from Sonning cutting to Reading, the nearest point to Elstree, the helicopter's base. On the day of the run, 17 October 1971, the helicopter was unable to take off because of thick ground fog. The sun was there all right at 2,000 feet but it was going to be a neck-and-neck business if the fog burned off before the train had gone too far and too fast to be caught. As she left Olympia at 10.45 a.m. we sat on the ground with the helicopter pilot, ringing the stations on the route to check her time of passing and praying for a delay. All seemed lost and the train was already through the Sonning cutting when miraculously the fog lifted enough for us to scrape into the air within the legal limits of visibility. We took off in a scramble – flew at maximum speed to cut off the curve of the line from London and caught the train just as she left Didcot. There for a few minutes, in a brief spell of brilliant sunshine, under the vigilance of the London Air Traffic Controller and with some heart-warming teamwork from the pilot and cameraman, we managed to get a spectacular sequence of extremely low level aerial pictures of the train running under the bridges and behind the tall trees on the run into Swindon. Just as we were forced to climb back to a safe 1,500 ft. at the edge of the town the white banner of steam faded from the bright light under the pall of the fog.

In the *Steam Horse : Iron Road* series as it was first broadcast the two programmes on early and late locomotives were separated by a programme equally essential to a broad view of railway history – 'The Laying of the Lines'. There is already a sizeable library of books on various aspects of the subject and there are no doubt as many more to come. In the first twenty years after the opening of the Liverpool and Manchester Railway 5,000 miles of track had been laid in Britain alone, the skeleton of our present national railway system. By 1870 it had risen to almost 16,000 miles, most of it double. This was followed by many thousands of miles more when the railway went out from its native shores to conquer the world.

From the very beginning laying the line was engineering on an heroic scale. The first modern inter-city passenger carrying steam railway, the Liverpool and Manchester line, involved its engineer, George Stephenson, in the first railway tunnel at Edge Hill and a formidably deep cutting through rock at Olive Mount. It also presented him with one of the most serious obstacles ever encountered by any railway builder anywhere in the world – the four-mile stretch of the 'impassable' peat bog, Chat Moss, on the South Lancashire plain. After his reassuring success the lines began to proliferate across the land. A whole generation of gifted powerful men seemed to be waiting in the wings for the cue to take the stage, especially Robert Stephenson, Locke, Vignoles, Brunel and Cubitt. Between them they transformed the old landscape of rural England – the landscape we can still glimpse from the work of painters like Constable and Cotman and Joseph Wright of Derby – with cuttings, tunnels, embankments, bridges and viaducts.

In spite of some early anti-railway hostility, whipped up by road and canal interests who stood to lose by the new system, there was no conservation lobby to inhibit the sweeping plans of the great engineers and there seemed nothing they dared not attempt. Intent on exploitation of the landscape, they managed, miraculously, to enhance it with a staggering quantity of engineering masterpieces. Even today an unromantic diesel or electric locomotive hauling, perhaps, a train of bulk fluid containers, can catch at the heart as it crosses a graceful bridge or a viaduct spanning a wide valley on repeated slender arches.

To feature particular achievements over so many thousands of miles and so many years of effort meant making an entirely arbitrary choice. O. S. Nock, writer of many books on railway history, was offered the task of making his own personal selection of works in each major category. His choice determined our filming locations and incidentally reminded us that the risk has not yet left the railway business. We discovered that only for an hour or so on each side of noon, would the sunlight we wanted penetrate the depths of Tring cutting, the great scar in the Chilterns made by Robert Stephenson's original London to Birmingham line. Guarded by an escort in day-glow markings we took close-up shots of passing trains, inches away from the line, where the powerful air blast from a 100 m.p.h. electric locomotive meant bracing both camera and cameraman. And we could have used mountaineers' ropes to hold us as we leaned into the turbulent hill-lift when a southerly gale hit the White Cliffs high above Cubitt's tunnels on the South Eastern line between Folkestone and Dover. For good measure we picked our way on planks and girders high above the fast-moving waters of the Menai Strait as we filmed reconstruction work on the great tubular sections, damaged beyond repair by the fire of May 1970, on Robert Stephenson's marvellous Britannia Bridge.

The laying of the lines, one of the essential ingredients of our technological view of railway history, was the practical achievement of the phenomenal boom in railway companies that marked the years of the 'railway mania'. The lines were built for profit as company by company their promotors banded together to secure the necessary Bill from Parliament that would approve the route, authorise the compulsory purchase of the required land, and enable them to raise capital by selling shares.

The financial risks of the early lines were taken on the certainty of an assured market for their services. Their apparently easy success spelt out the directions for a host of followers along what promised to be a royal road to riches. Suddenly it was imperative to build railways from everywhere to everywhere else. The flurry and excitement of the boom, of the physical drama of railway building and the financial excitement of wild speculation in shares, concealed the sad truth that there were soon more railways than the available traffic could ever support at a profit. The collapse, in 1849, of the speculative bubble that had been maintained by George Hudson, whose promotions earned him the title of 'The Railway King', was a clear signal of danger that was soon forgotten. Races, rivalries and duplication of routes led inevitably to a spate of failures and takeovers, culminating in the twentieth century in rationalisation of more than 120 once proud and ambitious separate companies into a few larger groups. All the same the vision or avarice of the early promoters – how you read their achievements depends on your own political colour – succeeded in attracting and concentrating the capital required to build a nationwide railway network where it had proved impossible, politically

and economically, to raise money for anything but a few moderately efficient roads. It is ironic that the great new road system, that is draining the life-blood of profit away from the railways, discovered from them its justification and its latest advances in engineering – its separated up and down carriageways, its junctions, its fast and slow lanes, its 'flyovers', its computerised traffic control and centralised signalling. Some historians have been tempted to speculate whether an intelligent and imaginative road programme, introduced when the first steam road vehicles were being priced out of existence by hostile turnpike tolls, might have made the whole railway investment unnecessary!

For our approach the material we needed was the visible evidence left by the pre-group years, when each company, large or small, had not only its own lines but often its own locomotive design, its own livery of sparkling paintwork, its own style and service. Some small lines have managed to find support for preservation and their rolling stock and special character can be enjoyed by enthusiasts and tourists. Much more often when individual company lines were 'absorbed' into the larger systems their individual qualities were lost and it was a chancy business whether their fascinating and charming old locomotives found their way into the transport museums instead of into the breaker's yards. A programme on the 'corporate personalities' of the old companies would offer more than a catalogue of their names and routes. C. Hamilton Ellis, who has written so well on the theme, was able to bring us a wealth of accumulated company lore and an artist's appreciation of the fine decoration that embellished many old engines. His own nostalgic paintings, meticulously detailed as to livery and date, are in a way, a personal salute to the confidence and belief that the Victorians expressed in elaborating their railway design.

All of these programme subjects are obviously inter-connected, each contributing to the better understanding of the others. But television viewers do not usually study the content of a series with the dedication of students facing an examination. Between weekly programmes they spend seven days ranging over other facts, other stories, other images. Except in the grip of a dramatic serial they may not need, or even want, a strict chronology or structure. Watching the steady growth of the railways along a broad front of advance would not, therefore, have any particular value and individual programmes could profit from their detachment to pick out, one by one, significant elements of the story, tracing their progress against the general growth. There were a number of such elements that seemed to be worthwhile and although in the broadcast series technical considerations determined their sequence, it is possible in this book, by changing their relative position, to alter the emphasis on the historical links that bind them together.

One subject of this kind was railway accidents – not the recent ones but accidents far enough removed in time for it to be possible to survey the causes and consequences without too heavy an emotional load of grief and horror. The purpose was not to shiver over the drama of the events themselves but to see how accidents arose out of the very advance of technology. If railway history has taught us anything on this matter it is that if an accident *can* happen, sooner or later it *will* happen. So the disasters of the past have not only built up a bank of what could be called 'precautionary information' but they have established a permanent social attitude towards safety in all our machinery. In the past as today, the enemies of safety were growing operational complexity, unwillingness on the part of employers to spend 'unnecessary' money, and the occasional 'sloppy' practises of employees. The inspecting officers of the Board of Trade set a shining example of devotion to duty, elucidation of the true facts, and disinterested efforts to protect the safety of the travelling public.

Our contributor, O. S. Nock, spent his entire professional life in the specialised business of railway signalling equipment and he is therefore an acknowledged world expert on many aspects of railway safety. Once again, therefore, he was in a very good position to suggest appropriate examples of accidents for the programme. He chose

for detailed demonstration three events in which the fatal results were due to three completely different kinds of failure – to the faulty design of brakes in the case of the runaway train at Armagh, to signal failure (again an unsuspected design fault) when the *Flying Scotsman* ran into the wreckage of an earlier collision at Abbots Ripton, and the failure of a signalman to keep track of a complex movement operation at Hawes Junction. By reconstructing the layout of tracks and trains with models it was possible to show, stage by stage, how an 'unlucky' technical failure, often compounded by human error, built up into a disaster and how from each catastrophe a technical advance was gained.

The history of the railway carriage, though totally different in mood, reflects a similar hard-won evolution. This is a second subject on which C. Hamilton Ellis has established an encyclopaedic knowledge. Since the traveller and his or her needs can have changed very little in the first hundred years of railway history it is strange that it took that long for the basic necessities of comfortable travel to be provided. It is even stranger in these egalitarian times to discover that almost all these basic necessities *were* available, from the very beginnings of railway operation, but only to distinguished personages and first-class passengers. It was not simply that they were too expensive to be offered to the 'poorer class of persons', the ordinary travellers, it was rather that it was considered socially inappropriate. Certain 'differentials' of luxury had apparently to be observed and it was as much social development as technical advance that brought 'comfortable carriage' within reach of all, made it in fact a matter of competition between rival transport systems in soliciting the patronage of the fare-paying customer.

To illustrate the high level of excellence in Victorian carriage-work we were able to show, for the first time, colour film sequences of the details of the interior of Queen Victoria's royal coach of 1869. The original interior decorations of blue watered silk are now so frail that the Curator of the Transport Museum at Clapham, Mr J. H. Scholes, could not permit us to carry lights for filming into the carriage and it proved very difficult to provide sufficient light from outside without risk of over-heating the dark maroon paintwork, also original, of the exterior. Soon this and other famous carriages will be leaving London, where we filmed them, and going to York, and our programme may well be the last opportunity of seeing them in a familiar setting.

At first sight our next programme, on the architecture of railway stations, can be linked very neatly to the artistic parts of those on carriages and company livery. Old stations have great charm, especially the idiosyncratic rural ones, and companies could give expression to their 'corporate images' in their style of building and decoration. Occasionally they even indulged in some fantasies to please either themselves or the local gentry. When 'stationary engine' houses were being built to serve the short-lived experiments of the 'atmospheric railway' one squire insisted that the new building should be erected in the style of a gothic chapel. (Actually one such engine house later conveniently *became* a non-conformist chapel, when its railway days were over.) Maybe in these days of green belts and jealous land conservation a Gothic chapel would offend the sensitive eyes as much or even more than an engine house! But all railway architecture does not possess these period overtones and a case can be made for linking it to the more robust monuments of the civil engineering undertaken in the laying of the lines.

Fire, earthquake or war can destroy bridges and viaducts and changes in traffic density or routing can render them inadequate or obsolete, but stations, however meritorious simply as buildings, are far more vulnerable to destruction. Built in astonishing numbers over a short period, they made a considerable contribution to the general prosperity brought by the railways. Now the private motor-car has enlarged the catchment area for individual access points to the lines and many small country stations are no longer required, quite apart from all those closed in the recent general reduction of track. Some of them have found immediate use as dwelling-houses and some of them indeed were never any more than the station

master's home adapted for ticket-selling, with the possible addition of a waiting room. Not all of them, however, were built in the vernacular style by a local contractor; some of them are surviving examples of the work of famous architects engaged by the railway companies and are well worth the effort and cost of preservation.

Tragically, many interesting and even distinguished smaller station buildings are already being left to decay. Once they are far advanced into ruin, restoration costs a fortune and without wishing to turn modern Britain into an open-air museum, it seems like an investment in the future of the tourist industry, if nothing more, to save these buildings.

The fate of the small, unpretentious stations is just as likely to overtake the big city mainline through-stations or terminals. Some magnificent structures are already out of service and converted to other purposes with all the risks of low maintenance and damage. When they were built they often stood on cheap land on the edge of the city but now, after a century of urban expansion and rocketing land-values, they hold out a constant temptation for profitable redevelopment. There have already been some glaring examples of unnecessary destruction (some people call it vandalism) and the real safeguard for major buildings if the railway or local authorities are insensitive to their value is a protective climate of informed public opinion.

The railway architecture programme was unusual in the series in having two main contributors: small country stations were dealt with by David Lloyd who is a well-known writer and lecturer on this topic, while the great city stations were treated by Sir James Richards, a former architectural critic of *The Times* and editor of the *Architectural Review*. Reflecting this division of labour they have written two separate chapters.

The final chapter in this book, 'Uphill and Round the Bend', encompasses material that sustained two television programmes though it confirms the original production intention that one programme should be devoted to the specialised railways – to mountain trains and to the articulated locomotives

13

that started from small beginnings and became the great trans-continental carriers of Australia, Africa and the U.S.A. In the event a lucky spell of fine weather when we were filming in North Wales allowed us to get more and better footage of the Snowdon, Festiniog and Vale of Rheidol railways than we could have dared to predict. At the same time the Swiss Railways completed a film on their own mountain railways that released to us an unexpected quantity of new material that it would have been uneconomic for us to shoot ourselves. We also, in the course of our researches, unearthed enough film on foreign railways to enable us to make two complete programmes instead of the one we had first planned.

The content of 'Uphill and Round the Bend' was divided, then, into two programmes 'Up the Mountain' and 'Round the Bend'. The first featured the locomotives of the Rigi, Pilatus, Mt. Washington and Snowdon Railways, while in the second the 'great little trains of Wales' ushered in these star performers of the past, the mighty Garratts and Mallets, including the largest and most powerful locomotive ever built, capable of hauling a loaded freight train five *miles* long — the incomparable *Big Boy* of the Union Pacific.

This book has been written, partly in response to requests from many viewers, as a memento of the original *Steam Horse : Iron Road* series. Its chapters are not reproductions of the television programme scripts but more detailed essays on the same subjects by the hands of the same contributors. Like the series it does not aspire to be a definitive or indeed comprehensive treatment of an enormous subject. It is, rather, an anthology and as such I hope it will be enjoyed.

Trevithick's 'London' carriage, from a painting by Terence Cuneo

The early locomotive

J. T. van RIEMSDIJK

The first steam locomotive for use on a railway was built in England by Richard Trevithick in 1802. Trevithick was able to build a locomotive because he had invented a new type of steam engine which was light and compact in relation to its power output. Its design owed a great deal to the pioneers of the stationary steam engine – to Denis Papin who in 1690 had made a small model which was the first steam engine to use a piston in a cylinder; to Thomas Newcomen, the true inventor of the industrial steam engine which caused the Industrial Revolution, and from its first use in 1712 onwards had helped to bring about the improvements in technology which made the later developments possible; to James Watt, whose improvements to the Newcomen engine from 1769 onwards had included the double-acting principle (which causes the piston to exert power in both directions of motion) and the conversion of reciprocating motion, which sufficed for the early pumping engines, to rotary motion for driving machines. However, the engines of Newcomen and Watt were structurally dependent on the massive engine houses into which they were built, and using 'kettle' steam at a pressure scarcely above that of the atmosphere they depended upon the creation of a vacuum for their working. The vacuum was produced by condensing steam on one side of the piston, while atmospheric pressure, either of the air itself (in the case of Newcomen engines) or of low pressure steam (in the case of the Watt engine) was brought to bear upon the opposite side.

The small pressure difference made it necessary to have a very large piston, and the condensing apparatus, though very different in Newcomen and Watt engines, required in all cases a cumber-some tank and piping. The first attempt at a self-propelling steam engine which came anywhere near to success was the artillery tractor of Nicholas Cugnot, which dispensed with condensation altogether, using steam at a higher pressure on one side of the piston, and allowing this to escape into the atmosphere after use, which meant that atmospheric pressure opposed the steam pressure, but provided that the steam pressure was high enough, this did not matter. This was precisely the concept behind Trevithick's engines, but Cugnot, a contemporary of Watt, was well in advance of his time and was unable to use a sufficiently high steam pressure to make a success of his two tractors. All the same, considering the date of his experiments, 1770-1, it must be conceded that his ideas were remarkable. His boilers had internal fireboxes and flues, and he used two single-acting cylinders driving the front wheel by means of ratchets.

When Trevithick contemplated using high pressure steam, just at the end of the eighteenth century, he felt that the improvements in the quality of iron manufacture since Newcomen's day freed him from the necessity of using 'kettle' steam, as Watt was still doing, and decided to go for 'strong' steam at pressures up to 50 lb on the square inch. This earned him the hostility of Watt, who was his employer (and by this time a somewhat reactionary influence as another employee, William Murdock, had discovered earlier) in spite of which Trevithick persisted and obtained more economical working with engines fitted with condensers. Seeing a growing need for lightweight steam engines for agricultural work, he decided that he could afford to dispense with the condenser. With the pressure of steam he was using, even without a condenser,

15

there would be about four times the effective pressure on the piston, as compared with an ordinary Watt engine. This meant that the piston could be only half the diameter for the same thrust. He designed a small and very strong cast-iron boiler, with the cylinder partly inside it and the crankshaft bearings and other components all bolted onto it. It was in fact both boiler and main structure, and with this engine Trevithick originated the idea of the power-to-weight ratio which has become so significant in the development of the motor-car, and so vital to that of the aeroplane.

Trevithick very quickly made several road vehicles, of which perhaps the most developed was his 'London' carriage, which incorporated a horizontal boiler surmounted by a stage-coach body. The cylinder was also horizontal, and the crankshaft was geared to the road wheels. The arrangement was that used in his Pen-y-Darran locomotive, and in this period of experimentation it is quite likely that many components were used in more than one machine. The road vehicles were successful in a purely technical sense, but Trevithick abandoned them because the roads themselves were very poor, and the steam engines were extremely noisy and unsuitable for use on a public road, especially if there were horses around. They were noisy because the steam was not yet used expansively, which meant that when it was exhausted into the air it produced an explosive sound, quite unlike that of the steam locomotives of later years and probably more like that of an unsilenced motor-cycle engine. Trevithick was in fact obliged to fit silencers to his engines, essentially the same as those fitted to motor cars today.

So it was on the railways that Trevithick's high pressure non-condensing engine eventually found its most important use, for right up to the present time the vast majority of steam locomotives have been of this type, and it has been on the railways that the general public has become familiar with the sight and sound of the steam engine and has understood something of its simple and robust engineering.

In Trevithick's time it was already common practice to lay rails along tracks where heavy loads had to be transported and this was already called a 'railway'. In Britain it was over a century old, and elsewhere its origins could be traced back a good deal further. At the beginning of the nineteenth century the lines were all private ones connected with industry, so not only could Trevithick find a good surface for running his engines on, but he could also do so without arousing public hostility. The principal motive power of these early industrial lines was the horse, and it was as a 'steam horse' that the first Trevithick locomotive was tried at Coalbrookdale in 1802. No more fitting place could have seen this first effort, because no ironworks has a surer place in the history of the rise of modern industry than the works at Coalbrookdale, where, in 1709, iron was first successfully smelted in a coke-fired furnace, and where seventy years later the first iron bridge was made and erected to span the River Severn. The railway at Coalbrookdale was perhaps the first in Britain to be equipped with iron rails in place of wooden ones, so it was suitable for the trials of a locomotive which must have weighed nearly four tons.

The little that is known of that first locomotive and its trials amounts to this: there was an accident, possibly fatal, followed by an enquiry and the abandonment of the experiment.

In February 1804 the second and most famous of Trevithick's locomotives started its short career at the Pen-y-Darran ironworks, near Dowlais in South Wales. Its planned duty was to haul ten ton loads of iron along the nine miles of railway to Abercynon where it could be loaded onto canal boats. The owner of the Pen-y-Darran ironworks, Samuel Homfray, laid a wager of 500 guineas with a neighbouring ironmaster, Anthony Hill, that it would perform better than a horse. The wager was won by a handsome margin, the engine handling loads of twenty-five tons of iron without difficulty, travelling at five miles per hour, and able to surmount gradients as steep as 1 in 36. It even managed to do the round trip without replenishment of the water in the boiler. A point of special interest is Trevithick's observation, in a letter dated 20

The Stephenson family, George Stephenson is seated, with his son Robert standing on the right. The locomotive in the background is typical of the period 1809–12, when George Stephenson was chief engineman at the Killingworth Colliery

The opening of the Liverpool and Manchester Railway. The Duke of Wellington's ceremonial carriage is on the left, and there are five Rocket type locomotives visible in the picture

February, that 'the fire burns much better when the steam goes up the chimney than – when the engine is idle'. Here we have the observation which was to result in virtually all locomotives puffing their exhaust steam out of the chimney, to draw up the fire, and thereby to provide themselves with the splendid canopy of white steam, or the less splendid canopy of black smoke, which was to catch the eye in the landscape for more than a century and a half as well as the puffing sound that was to become the authentic voice of the locomotive, and indeed of the railway.

The exploits of this engine were the subject of the first published account of the running of a steam train, which appeared in *The Cambrian* on 24 February, 1804:

. . . the novel application of steam, by means of this truly valuable machine, was made use of to convey along the Tram road ten tons long weight of bar-iron, from Pen-y-Darran ironworks to the place where it joins the Glamorganshire Canal, upwards of nine miles distance; and it is necessary to observe, that the weight of the load was soon increased from ten to fifteen tons, by about seventy persons riding on the trams, who, drawn thither (as well as many hundreds of others) by invincible curiosity, were eager to ride at the expense

of this first display of the patentee's abilities in this country. To those who are not acquainted with the exact principle of this new engine it may not be improper to observe that it differs from all others yet brought before the public, by disclaiming the use of condensing water, and discharges its steam into the open air . . .

This locomotive weighed five tons, and was used on a plateway – a form of railway which enjoyed a brief popularity at the end of the eighteenth century, because the wagons had no flanges on the wheels and thus could be used on the road also. The flange was transferred to the rails, which might have strengthened them but for the fact that it was on one side. In fact, the 'tram plates' as they were called, were weaker than edge rails, and also collected dirt as rails do not. Trevithick's locomotive broke a great many plates during its trials, and was also far more powerful than needed, so he planned a smaller example, but this does not appear to have been built.

The exact form of the Pen-y-Darran locomotive is unknown, but there are sufficient details to be found in contemporary letters and other sources for it to be possible to reconstruct it in model form with a fair degree of certainty, and the Science Museum in London has a model based on such

A model of Trevithick's Pen-y-Darran locomotive in the Science Museum

research. In the same museum there is a Trevithick stationary engine and boiler and also the original drawing of what seems to have been Trevithick's third locomotive, built at Gateshead for Christopher Blackett of the Wylam Colliery, in 1805. These give the best possible evidence for the form of the boiler, which had an internal firebox with a single horizontal flue of large diameter, which doubled back to emerge from the boiler at the base of a tall chimney, at the side of the firebox door. The Gateshead built locomotive is the one for which the best evidence is available. It was built for use on wooden edge rails, but after a successful trial (and, one imagines, in view of what happened later at Wylam Colliery, a prolonged and thorough inspection) it was not accepted and was applied to stationary use.

Trevithick's last locomotive was variously known as the *London locomotive* and as *Catch me who Can*, and was also associated with the slogan 'Mechanical power subduing animal speed'. It was, in fact, an attempt to win public interest in the steam locomotive, and was set to run round a circular track not far from the present site of Euston station. It hauled an open four-wheeled carriage of the kind used for conveying wealthy women on social trips on summer afternoons, and tickets could be purchased for two shillings – quite a large sum which would buy a hundred miles of train travel at excursion rates a century later. This was the first occasion on which people bought tickets for

Richard Trevithick – and his last steam locomotive, Catch me who Can, *from a watercolour attributed to Thomas Rowlandson*

travelling on a steam train. A contemporary water-colour drawing, signed T. Rowlandson (and very much in that artist's style, though its authenticity has been doubted) gives a fair idea of the locomotive, though clearly the artist had no idea of how this might work. The tickets, some of which still exist, depict this engine more clearly, and it appears identical in everything but its wheels with the stationary engine in the Science Museum. This stationary engine was rescued by F. W. Webb, the eminent engineer of the railway which owned

A model of Catch me who Can *in the Science Museum*

Euston station. In 1808, when *Catch me who Can* chased its tail on its circle of rails where University College now stands, Euston station did not exist. All the same, there is a distinct possibility that the engine Webb rescued is a reconstruction of what was once Trevithick's last locomotive.

The London demonstration produced no orders for locomotives and Trevithick turned his attention elsewhere. So the inventor of the steam locomotive derived no profit from his invention. His place in history is assured by many other important developments in steam power, and he was not always so unsuccessful in a material sense as with his experiments in steam locomotion, but the locomotive is undoubtedly his greatest and most momentous contribution to the modern world.

The first commercially successful locomotives were built in 1812 for the Middleton Colliery Railway near Leeds. An important improvement first incorporated in them was the provision of two cylinders, with the cranks at right angles, so that the locomotive was self-starting in all positions, and the action was far smoother. Probably 95 per cent of all steam locomotives have had two cylinders, with the cranks at right angles. Only for the highest powers has it been necessary to use three or four, and ones with six or eight have been confined to a very few, though successful, special purpose machines. The builder of the Middleton engines was the firm of Fenton, Murray and Wood, Matthew Murray being the designer, but these engines had one feature due to John Blenkinsop, the colliery superintendent, and this was the provision of a toothed wheel on the locomotive

19

which engaged with a rack formed on one of the running rails. Blenkinsop was thus the originator of the type of railway used for climbing mountains and other very steep gradients, the sole British example of which is the Snowdon Railway. The Middleton locomotives had their two cylinders vertical and sunk into the boiler, like the single one of *Catch me who Can*. They drove the toothed wheel, not the four carrying wheels. The exhaust steam was not at first passed up the chimney to induce a draught in the fire, but went straight into the air via a silencing box. Pictures of the railway made some years after the first appearance of the locomotives suggest that the exhaust steam was then diverted to the chimney as Trevithick had shown.

There were four of these machines, and they were capable of hauling 100 tons on the level at $3\frac{1}{2}$ m.p.h. They replaced 50 horses (and incidentally put 200 men out of work). They continued in use until 1834, when one of them exploded, but it seems to have been the last survivor of its kind, and locomotives of more recent and orthodox design took over the line, which still exists. A few similar machines were built for other railways, and attempts were made to copy the type in Germany, but at that time German technology was not able to make a success of so advanced a machine.

In spite of Trevithick's success, or perhaps because the details of his locomotives were unknown and only the general outlines of his designs transmitted by hearsay, there was a prevalent belief around 1812 that a smooth iron wheel could only get a small grip upon a smooth iron rail. Thus William Chapman had the idea of a locomotive which proceeded by gripping a stationary chain lying between the rails, and William Brunton built one or more which were provided with steam operated legs pushing at the rear end in the manner of Sisyphus rolling his stone uphill. However, William Hedley, viewer or superintendent of Wylam Colliery was, in his own words, 'forcibly impressed with the idea that the weight of an engine was sufficient for the purpose of enabling it to draw a train of loaded wagons'. As pointed out

earlier, Trevithick's third locomotive was built for the Wylam Colliery to the order of the owner, Christopher Blackett, and it seems unlikely that his viewer, Hedley, was not present at the trials. Those trials must have given Hedley the basis of his forcible impression, but to quote him again, 'To determine this important point I had a carriage constructed . . . loaded with different parcels of iron, the weight of which had previously been ascertained; two, four, six etc. loaded coal wagons were attached to it, the carriage itself was moved by the application of men at the four handles and in order that the men might not touch the ground, a stage was suspended from the carriage at each handle for them to stand upon. I ascertained the proportion between the weight of the experimental carriage and the coal wagons at that point when the wheels of the carriage would surge or turn round without advancing it . . . This experiment, which was on a large scale, was decisive of the fact that the friction of the wheels of an engine carriage upon the rails was sufficient to enable it to draw a train of loaded coal wagons.'

This admirably scientific experiment established the predominant principle of railway traction up to the present day, and only with the development of the linear electric motor is there any prospect, and that a remote one, of its supersession on a large scale.

Hedley made a model of his experimental carriage, which is now in the Science Museum in London, as is his first successful locomotive *Puffing Billy,* which is the oldest locomotive in existence and the first commercially successful one to depend on the factor of adhesion between a smooth wheel and a smooth rail. It was not actually Hedley's first locomotive. This was built upon the experimental carriage and was a failure. It is possible that *Puffing Billy* was also built on the experimental carriage, as it started life as a four wheeled engine, with flangeless wheels for use on the plateway, and, then as now, had the sort of geared drive from external cranks which is to be seen in the model of the experimental carriage. It was soon altered to travel upon eight wheels,

Puffing Billy,
*showing the
driving
position*

because of the poor state of the plateway, and this involved further gearing and some flexibility, lateral as well as vertical, of the wheel arrangement. It reverted to four wheels, but with flanges, when the railway was relaid with edge rails in 1828.

The precise date of *Puffing Billy* is uncertain, but probably late in 1813. In its construction Hedley was assisted by Jonathan Foster, enginewright at the colliery, and by Timothy Hackworth, the blacksmith, who later became one of the most notable pioneer locomotive builders. *Puffing Billy* had

a Trevithick type boiler, of wrought iron plates. The mechanism was clearly inspired by the experimental carriage, cranks on the underframe being geared to the wheels and operated by what amounted to a type of beam engine on each side of the boiler. Thus there was a cylinder on each side, with its piston rod working upwards to oscillate the end of a lengthways beam which was pivoted at the chimney end of the boiler. From the middle of each beam hung a connecting rod attached to the crank, the cranks on the two sides of the engine

Puffing Billy at work, c. 1860

being at right angles to ensure self-starting. From the beams also depended tappet rods for the cylinder valve gear, and a boiler feed-pump drive.

The sight of this engine in motion must have been awe inspiring. As it advanced at walking pace, the two beams on each side of the boiler waved up and down, neither in unison nor yet in contrary motion but in that sequential movement which results from the cranks being set at right angles. The various rods ascended and descended, and the large and somewhat crude gears between the wooden frames no doubt ground together noisily. The engineman, probably once accustomed to leading teams of horses on the same duty, would as gladly lead his steam horse on foot as ride upon it, and might mount and dismount at either end of the boiler for various purposes. For 48 years this engine worked a five mile railway between the colliery and the river, pulling 50 tons of coal at walking pace. Two similar engines were built immediately after it: *Wylam Dilly* now in the Royal Scottish Museum, and *Lady Mary,* which has disappeared. All three were retired when the gauge of the railway was altered from 5 ft. to the standard

4′ 8½″ in 1861. Their extraordinary longevity, for so early and experimental a type of machine, entitles them to be regarded as the first wholly successful railway locomotives.

Within months of *Puffing Billy's* completion, George Stephenson completed *his* first locomotive, and to Stephenson must go the credit for all the progress in locomotive design in the next ten or twelve years. The Middleton and Wylam engines were at work, but no advances or new construction took place at either place, as far as can be made out. But in this period Stephenson made – by his own account – about sixteen locomotives. He was the enginewright at Killingworth Colliery, near Wylam, where he built stationary engines and equipped the railway with four or five locomotives, subsequently supplying them for other railways as well.

His first locomotive, the *Blücher,* completed at the end of July 1814, was very similar to the Middleton engines, though followed Hedley in having the drive to smooth wheels, via an arrangement of gearing. The two cylinders were vertical, and partly inserted into the top of the boiler, as at Middleton. To increase the grip upon the track, the

Stephenson's colliery locomotive, c. 1820

front wheels of the tender were driven by a chain from the rear wheels of the engine, but this device was found to be unnecessary. However, it is of interest, because Stephenson's next type of locomotive used a chain to couple the two axles together, and the gearing disappeared. The cylinders drove directly onto crank pins in the wheels, following the early example of Trevithick's *Catch me who Can*, and as the foremost cylinder, set in the boiler top, drove the front wheels, and the rear one similarly drove the rear wheels (the connecting rods being duplicated on the two sides of the boiler, at both ends) the chain served to preserve the correct right-angled setting of the cranks. He also conceived the idea of coupling axles by two horizontal coupling rods, connecting cranks arranged at right angles on each axle. This he planned to arrange between the wheels, necessitating cranked axles (later an extremely familiar feature of the steam locomotive) but when he eventually came to use this idea, he placed the coupling rods outside the wheels in the way which has been used ever since.

Stephenson supplied five locomotives to the Hetton Colliery and a number of others to various users, including a six-wheeled one to the Kilmarnock and Troon Railway, but the greatest triumph of his pioneering days was undoubtedly achieved on the Stockton and Darlington Railway.

The route of the Stockton and Darlington Railway was surveyed by George Stephenson himself, with the help of his son Robert, who was to prove no less great an engineer than his father. In fact Robert Stephenson is a clear example of that rare phenomenon, an hereditary genius. Robert's name was appended to the plans, an instance of that fatherly devotion which later caused the locomotive building enterprise to be known as Robert Stephenson and Company. The S. & D. R. was to be a public railway, both for goods and passengers, and this was something of an innovation, but its historic importance was further established by the decision to use steam locomotives for the first time on a public railway, though at first only for goods trains. The occasion of its opening, in 1825, is widely regarded as the beginning of the national railway system, the point where a private industrial conveyor system blossomed into a public service. For this occasion, the Stephensons built

A model of Stephenson's Locomotion, *Stockton and Darlington Railway; No. 1, 1825*

Locomotion, No. 1 on the books of the S. & D.R., and this famous locomotive still stands carefully preserved upon Darlington station.

From the technical point of view *Locomotion* is mainly interesting because it has outside coupling rods on its four wheels. In other respects it is much like the previous and well-tried Stephenson locomotives, for such an important event as the opening of the railway was not the moment for experiments. It is a large example of the type, but is none the less clearly a low-speed machine, the boiler of which, having a single large flue passing through from the rear of the boiler where it housed the fire, to the front where it joined the chimney, could not produce steam rapidly enough to permit of any rapid progress. However, it hauled a passenger train of sorts on the opening day, consisting mainly of open chauldron wagons designed for coal but full of enthusiastic supporters of the new enterprise. The only passenger vehicle was a sort of garden shed on wheels, provided for the important personages present, and the whole cheerful procession was preceded by a man on horseback waving a large flag.

From the time of the opening of the Stockton and Darlington Railway George Stephenson became more in demand as an engineer of railways, rather than just of locomotives. He rapidly became a national figure, widely admired and accepted in society, not only for his recognised genius but also for his great unpretentious personal charm. His son was deeply involved in the mechanical engineering of railways, and the locomotives of the S. & D.R. became the responsibility of the newly-appointed engineer of that railway, Timothy Hackworth, the Wylam blacksmith who had helped build *Puffing Billy*.

Even greater national interest was aroused five years later by the opening of the Liverpool and Manchester Railway, an occasion graced by the presence of the Duke of Wellington, then Prime Minister, and marred by a fatal accident to a distinguished Liverpool member of Parliament, William Huskisson, who stretching his legs when the train stopped at Parkside to take on water was knocked down by the *Rocket* locomotive before he could get back into the carriage. The Liverpool and Manchester was a main line – in fact the first part of the present day mainline system to be built, though the Stockton and Darlington line is still in operation, as a branch off the 'East Coast Route' to Scotland. The original intention of the directors of the L. & M.R. was to follow the practice of the S. & D.R. in using steam locomotives for goods trains, and conveying passengers in horse-drawn vehicles of road type, but fitted with flanged wheels. Steam locomotives were associated with heavy loads and low speeds, horses with light loads and high speeds – up to fifteen m.p.h. However, the engineer for the building of the line was George Stephenson, and he was not alone in suggesting that the high speed steam locomotive was a possibility. To resolve the matter, the directors advertised a locomotive trial, to take place at Rainhill near Liverpool.

The Rainhill Trials commenced on 6 October 1829. They were in fact a competition, for £500 was to be awarded to the best locomotive, which would then go into service on the railway, and other

Right: the poster of the Rainhill Trials

1829.

GRAND COMPETITION

OF

LOCOMOTIVES

ON THE

LIVERPOOL & MANCHESTER RAILWAY.

STIPULATIONS & CONDITIONS

ON WHICH THE DIRECTORS OF THE LIVERPOOL AND MANCHESTER RAILWAY OFFER A PREMIUM OF £500 FOR THE MOST IMPROVED LOCOMOTIVE ENGINE.

I.

The said Engine must "effectually consume its own smoke," according to the provisions of the Railway Act, 7th Geo. IV.

II.

The Engine, if it weighs Six Tons, must be capable of drawing after it, day by day, on a well-constructed Railway, on a level plane, a Train of Carriages of the gross weight of Twenty Tons, including the Tender and Water Tank, at the rate of Ten Miles per Hour with a pressure of steam in the boiler not exceeding Fifty Pounds on the square inch.

III.

There must be Two Safety Valves, one of which must be completely out of the reach or control of the Engine-man, and neither of which must be fastened down while the Engine is working.

IV.

The Engine and Boiler must be supported on Springs, and rest on Six Wheels; and the height from the ground to the top of the Chimney must not exceed Fifteen Feet.

V.

The weight of the Machine, WITH ITS COMPLEMENT OF WATER in the Boiler, must, at most, not exceed Six Tons, and a Machine of less weight will be preferred if it draw AFTER it a PROPORTIONATE weight; and if the weight of the Engine, &c., do not exceed FIVE TONS, then the gross weight to be drawn need not exceed Fifteen Tons; and in that proportion for Machines of still smaller weight—provided that the Engine, &c., shall still be on six wheels, unless the weight (as above) be reduced to Four Tons and a Half, or under, in which case the Boiler, &c., may be placed on four wheels. And the Company shall be at liberty to put the Boiler, Fire Tube, Cylinders, &c., to the test of a pressure of water not exceeding 150 Pounds per square inch, without being answerable for any damage the Machine may receive in consequence.

VI.

There must be a Mercurial Gauge affixed to the Machine, with Index Rod, showing the Steam Pressure above 45 Pounds per square inch; and constructed to blow out a Pressure of 60 Pounds per inch.

VII.

The Engine to be delivered complete for trial, at the Liverpool end of the Railway, not later than the 1st of October next.

VIII.

The price of the Engine which may be accepted, not to exceed £550, delivered on the Railway; and any Engine not approved to be taken back by the Owner.

N.B.—The Railway Company will provide the ENGINE TENDER with a supply of Water and Fuel, for the experiment. The distance within the Rails is four feet eight inches and a half.

THE LOCOMOTIVE STEAM ENGINES,

WHICH COMPETED FOR THE PRIZE OF £500 OFFERED BY THE DIRECTORS OF THE LIVERPOOL AND MANCHESTER RAILWAY COMPANY.

DRAWN TO A SCALE ¼ INCH TO A FOOT.

THE "ROCKET" OF MR ROBT STEPHENSON OF NEWCASTLE,

WHICH DRAWING A LOAD EQUIVALENT TO THREE TIMES ITS WEIGHT TRAVELLED AT THE RATE OF 12½ MILES AN HOUR, AND WITH A CARRIAGE & PASSENGERS AT THE RATE OF 24 MILES. COST PER MILE FOR FUEL ABOUT THREE HALFPENCE.

THE "NOVELTY" OF MESSRS BRAITHWAITE & ERRICSSON OF LONDON,

WHICH DRAWING A LOAD EQUIVALENT TO THREE TIMES ITS WEIGHT TRAVELLED AT THE RATE OF 20¼ MILES AN HOUR, AND WITH A CARRIAGE & PASSENGERS AT THE RATE OF 32 MILES. COST PER MILE FOR FUEL ABOUT ONE HALFPENNY.

THE "SANSPAREIL" OF MR HACKWORTH OF DARLINGTON,

WHICH DRAWING A LOAD EQUIVALENT TO THREE TIMES ITS WEIGHT TRAVELLED AT THE RATE OF 12½ MILES AN HOUR. COST FOR FUEL PER MILE ABOUT TWO PENCE.

locomotives which performed well might also be purchased, though they were not winners of the prize. The site was a stretch of level track, at the centre of which a sort of grandstand was erected, mainly for the accommodation of the ladies, and a band was engaged to play the favourite airs of the period. The trials went on for several days and there were over ten thousand spectators along the mile and a half of track.

The conditions which had to be met were, in summary, that the locomotive should consume its own smoke; that it should pull three times its own weight at 10 m.p.h., that the boiler pressure should not exceed 50 lb. per square inch (Trevithick's figure!); that it should not exceed $4\frac{1}{2}$ tons weight if on four wheels, or 6 tons if on six; and that it should repeat its performance often enough to establish its reliability. This last point was not published, but became clear at the trials.

The only locomotive which fulfilled all these conditions was the *Rocket*, entered by Robert Stephenson and Company. It hauled $12\frac{1}{2}$ tons at 10 m.p.h., and, without a load reached 30 m.p.h. It performed on several days, and must have covered something like 100 miles. It demonstrated in various ways that it was considerably more powerful than the conditions required, and its subsequent career on the railway confirmed the good impression it made at the trials. The Railway Company offered to buy two other locomotives which had done well. One of these was the *Sans Pareil* of Timothy Hackworth, which had not met the conditions, being slightly overweight, and had suffered a breakdown. Hackworth gladly sold the engine, but one aftermath of the trials was a life-long bitterness towards the Stephensons which Hackworth passed on to his son, and which even in the twentieth century has spread some confusion over the history of the early years of the steam locomotive. Today, the *Sans Pareil* stands close to

The Rocket, *1829 – now in the Science Museum*

The Novelty *locomotive, built by Braithwaite and Ericson in 1829. A full size reconstruction with original components*

Timothy Hackworth's Sans Pareil, *1829*

26

the *Rocket* in the Science Museum in London, in a mute, but to the discerning eye still unsuccessful, challenge to the verdict of 1829.

The other locomotive which the company offered to buy was not in fact sold. This was the *Novelty* of Braithwaite and Ericsson, a very light machine which had fulfilled the load and speed conditions – in fact it had exceeded the speed requirements handsomely – but had proved unreliable. This was a brilliant and original design, and its breakdowns were trivial matters due solely to the haste with which it had been prepared, but it was a concept of the locomotive which can now be seen to have been unsuitable for the enormous enlargement which time was to bring to the *Rocket* concept.

The only other entries were the wholly unsuccessful *Perseverance* of the unluckily named Mr Burstall, and a horse on a treadmill fitted to a wagon, entered by a Mr Brandreth and named *Cycloped*.

Until the appearance of the *Rocket* the locomotive had presented many different configurations of its various components. In a quarter of a century it had laboriously evolved into something which would work quite reliably, but had not found its definitive form and could even have disappeared, yielding place to cable traction or that ingenious curiosity, the atmospheric system. However, the *Rocket* assumed the definitive form, and all orthodox steam locomotives built since have been versions of it.

First, and most important, was the boiler, in which for the first time in a locomotive the fire was conducted through a large number of small tubes surrounded by water. At the same moment a great French engineer, Marc Seguin, was doing the same thing, but his boiler was not the type used on the *Rocket* and adopted generally. The *Rocket*'s boiler had a water-jacketed firebox at the rear end, and

A sketch of the Rocket's boiler, from the notebook of J. U. Rastrick, an observer at the Rainhill Trials

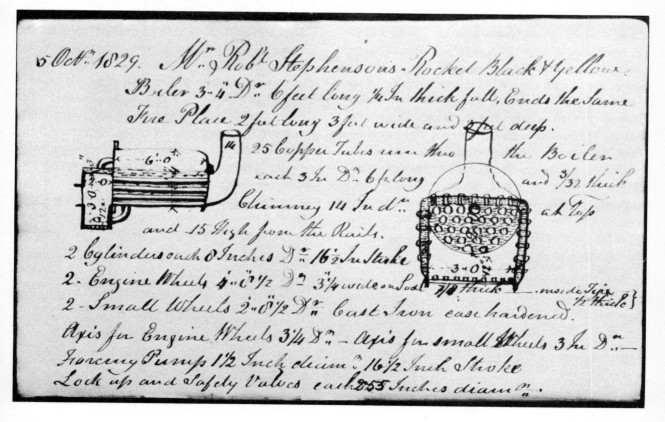

the fire was drawn through the twenty or so small tubes by the action of the exhaust steam turned up the chimney – as Trevithick had found beneficial. The steam nozzles in the chimney were slightly constricted, to increase their effect. This idea may have been due to Hackworth, who did this on the *Sans Pareil* to such effect that a great deal of fire was thrown out of the chimney during the Rainhill trials. The *Sans Pareil* did not have a multi-tubular boiler, the gas resistance of which would have prevented such a pyrotechnic display. It was the ability of the *Rocket* to boil water rapidly that gave it the decisive advantage over the *Sans Pareil*.

Another interesting thing about the *Rocket* was the simplicity of its driving mechanism. Gone were the gears of *Puffing Billy*, of course, but gone also were the beams and levers, and the double connecting rods of *Locomotion*. Even the coupling rods had gone, for the *Rocket* was not a coupled engine, and the large driving wheels were followed by small wheels under the rear end. The driving wheels had a diameter of 4′ 8½″ – equal to the distance between the rails which George Stephenson had fixed on the Killingworth Railway. They had crankpins set in their centres, to allow a piston stroke of 17″, and the cylinders were set up at an angle to the rear, rather too high, for they were lowered later, to prevent the engine rocking on its springs. Springs were still a novelty, and the *Sans Pareil* had none, but they would have been impossible anyway, because the cylinders were vertical on that engine, and also drove directly onto crankpins on the wheels, so they would simply have rocked the whole machine from side to side had there been springs.

At the grand ceremonial opening of the Liverpool and Manchester Railway there were present five locomotives of the *Rocket* type, the four new ones being named *Meteor*, *Comet*, *Arrow* and *Dart*. The *Rocket* weighed 4 tons 3 cwt. The others were a little heavier, having more tubes in the boiler, and their cylinders were more nearly horizontal. But the only alterations of any note made to the basic *Rocket* layout in the next few years – or indeed the next century and a half – were the inclusion of the water-jacketed firebox within the rear end of the boiler shell, rather than adding it on with connecting pipes, and moving the cylinders to the front of the engine. The practice of putting the cylinders under the smokebox, and driving onto a cranked axle instead of crankpins in the wheels themselves, which was for so long a feature of British locomotives, was never greatly favoured outside the British Isles and was eventually abandoned even within them, so this departure from the *Rocket* layout cannot be seen as an improvement but merely as an alternative.

The subsequent development of the *Rocket* design to twenty, thirty, or forty times the weight, and a hundred or more times the power, required an enormous number of changes in detail, in such things as the number of wheels and cylinders, in ways of using the steam, feeding the boiler with water and fuel, and developing new types of iron and steel and other metals. That these changes were wrought upon a design due above all to Robert Stephenson does not lessen the greatness of the engineers who created the great locomotive designs of later railway history, but an account of what they did must be left to another chapter.

Laying the lines

O. S. NOCK
B.Sc., C.Eng., F.I.C.E., F.I.Mech.E., F.I.R.S.E.

The Iron Road is with us still, very much a feature of the here and now. In spite of present-day problems it has a long and profitable future. Each day some three million of us travel by train, but my guess is that with few exceptions most of us take the line for granted. We may glance out of the window occasionally as the landscape races by, but the line itself, a tangible monument to some of the world's most daring engineers, is strictly a driver's eye view. But men had been laying lines long before Richard Trevithick and George Stephenson made the steam locomotive a practical proposition. They laid lines so that horses could pull a heavier load than on the deeply-rutted, poorly-surfaced roads of the eighteenth century. They used wooden rails at first, then various forms of iron castings. Gradients were at first relatively unimportant. Loads were hauled up steep hills by some of the earliest stationary steam engines, or simply by windlasses; but it was very different when the first self-propelled locomotives were introduced. To enable them to pull heavy loads the gradients had to be made as near level as possible. George Stephenson specified a maximum of 1 in 300, and so the colossal labour of building the earliest steam railways began. Cuttings had to be excavated; great embankments built; lengthy viaducts thrown across rivers and broad valleys, and long tunnels driven.

Everything had to be done by hand. A limited use of explosives was made for blasting rocks; horses and wheelbarrows were used for transport, when earth had been dug out, or rocks fragmented by blasting; but the entire labour of digging out excavations, of building bridges, stations and all else had to be done by hand. The labour force, which at times was enormous, was recruited from

A navvy – equipped for anything

the four corners of the British Isles: Irish seeking work away from their own famine-stricken country; Highland Scots, driven from their homeland by the notorious 'clearances' of the glens came to swell the ranks of the native English 'navvies' – men who were already versed in heavy earth works in constructing canals, 'navigators' as they were originally known.

The great engineering pioneers did the planning, and keen and bitter at times was the rivalry between the 'new men', like George Stephenson, who were both engine mechanics and civil engineers, and established professional men, like the Rennies, Francis Giles, and to a lesser extent the Brunels, father and son. But somehow men of the Stephenson stamp – George Stephenson himself, his brilliant son Robert, and Joseph Locke – applied a drive, a perception, a hard practical commonsense to the job of 'laying the lines' that seemed to be lacking in the established leaders of the profession. Brunel the younger was of course an exception. He was without question the most dashing and adventurous of them all; and although the details of their railway practice differed, so

29

Isambard Kingdom Brunel

greatly, the closest personal friendship came to be forged between Robert Stephenson, Locke and himself.

But the engineers, hard practical men though they were, could not directly control the huge labour forces that were involved. Robert Stephenson, for example, had the 112 miles of the London and Birmingham Railway; Brunel, 118 miles of the Great Western; Locke, the Southampton, the Grand Junction, the Lancaster & Carlisle, the Caledonian, and many more. The work had to be let to many contractors. Some were novices and fell down on the job, others struggled through, but with little profit to themselves; but one of the 'master' builders of the early railways – one who gained the most enviable reputation for superb workmanship, impeccable honesty, and masterly handling of his huge labour forces – was Thomas Brassey. He was sometimes referred to as the 'Navvy King'; but far from being a swashbuckling 'son of a gun' type of overseer he was a great Christian gentleman, who took his crack labour teams from success in the United Kingdom to many overseas railway constructional contracts, where they astonished the natives by the speed and vigour of their work.

One of the greatest of the early excavations was Tring cutting – dug for a length of nearly two miles, and ranging between 40 and nearly 100 ft. deep across the crest of the Chiltern Hills, in Hertfordshire. It was part of Robert Stephenson's London and Birmingham line. Today one can stand down in the depths of the cutting, and watch express after express, all electrically hauled, racing by at between 90 and 100 m.p.h.; but just imagine what it would have been like down there in 1838 when the line was being built and the whole place would have been swarming with men, thousands of them digging with nothing more than picks and shovels; digging this great excavation, moving the earth away with wheelbarrows and horses to drag the soil. They had to dig it out of the hard tenacious chalk, at the summit of the Chiltern Hills. The vast quantities of spoil were taken up the sides of the cutting by barrow runs made of planks. At Tring where there were thirty to forty of these runs up the steep chalk walls, they were the most spectacular and dangerous part of the excavation. The navvies worked in gangs, and the strongest man in the gang took the barrow; they called it 'making the running'. A rope was attached to the front of the barrow and usually another to the man's belt. At the top of the cutting the rope was taken through a pulley and a horse drew man and barrow up the muddy slippery plank. Falls were frequent and then the man had to jump clear of the load. But they got so agile that only one death from this cause occurred at Tring.

Robert Stephenson, son of the great pioneer, George, was the engineer, and ironically enough had he built the line about thirty or forty years later it would not have been necessary to have such an enormous cutting at all. In later years, when larger locomotives were available the railway could have been taken near to the top of the hills and most of this excavation avoided. When one thinks of the tremendous amount of spoil that was dug out of this cutting, the question arises as to what on earth they did with it all. Well, the engineers laid out the railway, as far as was possible so that the amount of spoil taken out of a cutting could be used for making embankments. Not far away to the north there is a very big embankment where a great deal of the spoil from Tring was conveyed.

One can be very sure however that the colossal labour of constructing the earth works was a mere incident to the great-hearted engineers who planned the railways -- they were verily the architects of a new age, and each problem, whether of technical construction, management of the mass-labour forces, or of the legal and Parliamentary battles to obtain sanction, was a challenge to the many-sided skills that they were learning to acquire. Today we can be amazed at the artistry that these pioneers – many of them entirely self-taught – displayed when it came to crossing rivers, or spanning broad valleys. Their structures not only transformed, but even ennobled the British landscape. There was no greater exponent of the artistic in railway construction than Isambard Kingdom Brunel, engineer of the Great Western Railway. If not one of the most spectacular of his works, certainly one of the most interesting was the bridge he built to carry the line across the River Thames at Maidenhead. There were three requirements that to a large extent dictated the design. First of all there must be no interruption of the waterway except for one pier right in the middle. The second factor which affected the design of the bridge was that the River Authorities insisted that the bridge should span the towing path. Those requirements dictated a certain width of arch. Now if the conventional form of

arch – well known at the time – had been used, the bridge would have been very much higher than it is today, and that would have meant the railway approach would have been much higher. The approaches from the level country on both sides would have been inclined, with tiresome gradients. And Brunel designed a very flat, very elegant arch – so flat that everyone thought it would fall down. It is built in red brick, and the usual form of wooden support shuttering was used during construction. The criticism of the design caused such concern among the directors of the Great Western Railway that Brunel was implored not to remove the shuttering when the bridge was finished. It was left up for over a year, until a great storm and flood blew it all down. Then everyone thought the bridge would fall down – except Brunel! The confidence in the design by his successors was shown when the line had to be widened in 1890, and the enlargement was made precisely to the original design. Walking along the towing path today, or passing slowly under in a boat, the sections that were added on either side of the original bridge can be clearly seen, the line being marked by a shallow buttress; and all the time the modern diesel-hauled expresses are roaring over it at between 90 and 100 m.p.h.

Every railway lover will have his own favourite bridge or viaduct, chosen because it is charming, or impressive, or simply because it is linked with some personal association. Whatever favourite

The building of Tring Cutting. A contemporary illustration by J. C. Bourne, clearly showing the barrow runs in a view looking south

any one may have they would, however, all agree that the unquestioned masterpiece of the age is the Britannia Bridge built by Robert Stephenson to cross the Menai Strait in 1849. Stephenson built the central tower for his bridge on the Britannia Rock, which stood conveniently in the middle of the strait. The other two main towers stood on dry land on the north and south banks. The girders that would carry the tracks were constructed in the form of tubes, one for each line. These immensely strong rectangular tubes were built at the waters edge so that they could be floated on pontoons out into the swift waters of the strait. The end of the girders were manoeuvred into specially made slots in the towers, and stage by stage they were jacked up and supporting masonry was built in beneath them. Robert Stephenson had more than his fair share of major anxieties. Having conceived the magnificent idea of the tubular bridge, there were times when the colossal size of the spans preyed on his mind. He said afterwards: 'Often at night I would lie tossing about, seeking sleep in vain. The tubes filled my head. I went to bed with them and got up with them. In the grey of the morning, when I looked across the Square, it seemed an immense distance to the houses on the opposite side. It was nearly the same length as the span of my tubular bridge!' Actually those central spans were 460 ft. long, and each tube weighed about 1,350 tons. On 23 May, 1970 the Great Britannia Bridge was damaged by fire and in deciding how to repair it today's engineers decided on the grounds of cost to replace the tubes by arched girders. The arches have reduced the clearance that the Admiralty once demanded for the tall masts of men-of-war navigating the strait on high tide. The slots in which the tubes were lifted up the towers have been masked and the tubes themselves, which were made of iron plates riveted together by Stephenson's men, were too badly distorted in the fire ever again to carry a train in safety; so they were scrapped. But as, once again, men were clambering among the high girders, the work on the new bridge, part demolition, part construction, allowed us to enjoy and appreciate anew the scale and sweep of this

fantastic achievement of Victorian engineering. The familiar shape of Stephenson's bridge has now vanished forever and we have seen for the last time the fascinating sight of the *Irish Mail* disappearing into the tube and reappearing on the farthest side.

Maidenhead and the Menai Strait are specialised cases of particular fascination; but the artistry of the early railway engineers is shown equally in great viaducts of many arches, such as Robert Stephenson's Royal Border Bridge over the river Tweed at Berwick, John Rennie's viaduct over the Sussex Ouse, near Hayward's Heath, on the Brighton line, and the beautiful viaduct by which William Cubitt carried the South Eastern Railway across the Foord Gap at Folkestone. The strength as well as the grace of these early railway viaducts was shown during World War II when a fine structure of twenty-seven arches at Brighton, built by John Rastrick in 1845, got a direct hit from a heavy bomb at the base of one of the piers. The line is 70 ft. above ground level, and only work of first class quality would have resisted such an attack without collapsing altogether. But here, it was only the pier actually hit that collapsed. The adjoining piers stood firm, while the rails – and amazingly one parapet – hung in mid-air across the gap. Five months after the 'incident' a temporary structure had enabled the line to be re-opened, and in four months the viaduct was completely restored.

Crossing valleys and rivers, where there were rocks or good solid ground to base the foundations was one thing; but very early in railway history engineers were faced with the crossing of a vast area of morass. Athwart the track of the Liverpool and Manchester Railway lay the notorious Chat Moss, an immense peat bog some twelve square miles in extent. It was a vast agglomerate of spongy vegetable swamp, the decay of ages – and George Stephenson planned to take the railway directly across it.

How deep the bog extended nobody seems to have known; but Stephenson's intention was to 'float' the road over the unstable portion, building

Brunel's Maidenhead Bridge, 1839

Floating the tubes into position during the building of the Britannia Bridge, 1849

the 'formation' on which the rails would be laid on a broad mattress of heather and brushwood laid across the bog. At first a footpath of heather was laid down so that men could walk beside the line of the railway without any fear of sinking; a temporary line of light railway was next put down to carry the wagons needed for conveyance of materials, and the ease with which the support for this line was made encouraged even the faintest of hearts. But the encouragement was short-lived. The drains could not be cut, on account of the quick silting up that followed, and in the softest parts the mattress of heather sank under the weight of the railroad itself – let alone any trains. On stretches like this it was the intention to run the line roughly at the level of the surface of the bog, and the places where subsidences occurred were corrected by packing more heather and more cakes of firm turf under the track itself. The drains were eventually consolidated by laying in tar barrels, as soon as the trench had been dug, eventually forming underground sewers of wood, instead of brick or iron. At the Manchester end a shallow embankment had to be formed. While in general the principle of the floating mattress was sufficient to carry the road and the trains, it was quite another matter, with the weight of earth required, to make an embankment. Men were employed to cut the driest moss in the neighbourhood, and this was duly tipped in to make the embankment. But each

load had gradually disappeared beneath the sedgy surface and weeks went by with nothing to show for this work. The local wiseacres began to shake their heads; even Stephenson's most trusted assistants grew uneasy, and the directors really grew alarmed. But the filling went on for week after week, until at last the embankment began to rise firm and solid. The appearance of it, when ultimately finished, was likened to a long ridge of tightly pressed tobacco leaf.

If bridges give scope for architectural distinction and result in creations that everyone can applaud, there is another form of railway engineering that, even less than crossing swamps, produces nothing for the eye to see, but which is perhaps the most demanding of all. That is tunnelling. There are many hundreds of tunnels on the railways of Britain, long ones, short ones, deep ones and shallow ones. Some are straight, and one can see through from end to end; others are curved, and there is one, near Kinghorn in Fife, where the surveys went wrong, and to correct it they had to put a zig-zag in the middle! In engineering terms one of the most hazardous was Kilsby, near Rugby, on Robert Stephenson's London and Birmingham line. The ridge here rose to some 160 ft. above the proposed level of the railway and a tunnel $1\frac{1}{2}$ miles long was needed.

Trial borings were made to ascertain the nature of the ground beneath the surface, and while these indicated shale and possible troubles with water they completely missed an extensive quicksand which existed beneath a bed of thick clay. It is interesting to speculate upon what tactics Robert Stephenson would have adopted if this extreme hazard had been known of earlier. As it was, the trial borings were enlarged to become working shafts, work was commenced in excavation and the quicksand was struck in the most dramatic and alarming manner. Without warning a deluge of water broke in, the works were flooded, and the men escaped only by swimming to the shaft. It was clear at once that water in such quantities could not be dealt with by any ordinary methods. Robert Stephenson sought his father's opinion, and while other engineers took the most pessimistic view and foretold complete abandonment, George Stephenson was steadfastness itself, as in his own predicament at Chat Moss, and counselled the use of more, more and still more pumps until the inward flow of water was mastered by sheer force of machinery.

Robert Stephenson as the responsible engineer and with his eye, no doubt, on the ultimate cost, tried a short cut, rather against his father's advice. He suggested running a driftway inwards from the open hillside, to strike the quicksand and drain the water away in that manner. It was tried, and the danger point was approached; then the workmen were all withdrawn from the driftway. Before long a roar was heard as of distant thunder. It was hoped that the water had burst in, but to everyone's surprise very little water made its way to the opening of the drift, and a cautious examination inside revealed that the water had certainly burst in, but in so doing had brought with it such a volume of sand that the whole driftway had been completely choked up! There was now nothing for it, but to pile on more and more pumps. During the next eight months the quantity of water removed averaged about 2,000 gallons per minute, and this was raised from a depth of 120 ft. Only by this colossal effort was it possible for the tunnel to be excavated, and eventually the overall cost came to more than £100 for every yard of railway through the tunnel. Today, even to the engine driver,

A working shaft for the construction of Kilsby Tunnel

Kilsby is just another tunnel. At 100 m.p.h. trains race through in a little more than a minute, now they are electric, and the line goes not just to Birmingham, but on to Manchester, Liverpool, and to Scotland. This particular part of the track, which has such a history behind it, is one of the busiest and most profitable stretches of all our railways.

In 1838, the same year that the London and Birmingham Railway was opened for traffic, the Manchester and Sheffield line was authorised. In profile the line can be likened to a huge gable, having its apex at the point where the railway was carried in a tunnel under the Pennines. And what a tunnel! At that time only two major tunnels had been driven in the construction of railways in England; of these the notorious Kilsby was 2,425 yds. long, while Box on the Great Western was 3,230 yds. Yet out in the wilderness of Woodhead Moor the Sheffield Railway was to pass through a tunnel 5,300 yds. long, blasted from the millstone grit of the Pennines. There were many difficulties at the start, and the engineer first appointed did not cope with the problems of organising the labour force; but in 1839 Joseph Locke was appointed and he quickly brought his clear brain

The western entrance to the Woodhead Tunnel. (From a photograph of 1903 in Great Central, Volume III *by George Dow)*

and superb organising skill to the great task of boring the first Woodhead Tunnel. His biographer tells us that the job of getting supplies forward was as bad as supporting the Crimean army before Balaclava! The contractors built shops of their own; sometimes the men were paid in food, and they camped in huts, quickly run up with loose stones and mud, and thatched with heather. They slept upon improvised truckle beds, twenty

Joseph Locke

together. It was a tremendous task. The tunnel was driven from two portals and five intermediate shafts, though no technical description of the work has survived. Driving in from the open hillside at the Woodhead portal the rocks are hard gritstone and sandstone at first, but then comes a thick slanting layer of that most treacherous rock formation – shale. Although there is no direct evidence it would seem certain that serious trouble with rock falls occurred; in any case during the six years it was under construction the first Woodhead Tunnel claimed the high casualty list of 28 killed, 200 seriously injured or disabled, and 450 lesser accidents.

Eventually it took six years to complete, and on 20 December 1845, it was ready for the Government inspection, by General Pasley of the Board of Trade. The execution of the work was first class, though against the naked rock-faces the castellated portals looked rather grim. At the western end the effect was heightened by some grotesque gargoyles over the entrance! General Pasley said that it was one of the finest pieces of engineering he had ever seen, and it was opened for traffic just before Christmas 1845. The shortsightedness of the

35

original decision to have a single tracked bore made purely to save costs, was apparent before the line had been opened two years! And while the engineering work to build a double line tunnel in the first place would not have been greatly more difficult, in 1847 the railway embarked upon the costly job of boring a duplicate tunnel alongside the older one, and this took a further five years to complete.

Of all the tunnelling works however, that which impresses me perhaps beyond all others, is the series on the South Eastern line, between Folkestone and Dover. This main line as laid out by William Cubitt was carried on a magnificently straight and easy course through the Weald of Kent, till Folkestone was reached. There, an abrupt change in the geological formation was obviously going to involve heavy engineering works, and the prospect of that range of lofty white cliffs, rising at times sheer from the sea, might well cause any engineer to pause and consider alternative ways of reaching Dover. Even before the chalk was entered there was the Foord gap. In crossing the greensand ridge that blocks in the eastern end of the Weald the railway approached Folkestone at high level, and a viaduct of nineteen arches having a maximum height of 100 ft. was necessary over the valley looking down to the narrow winding streets of Old Folkestone. Even then, although the white cliffs are near at hand, a ridge of hard gault outcrops the chalk before the undercliff of the Folkestone Warren is reached. The line is carried through the gault in the Martello Tunnel, so named from the watch tower of Napoleonic days on the shore nearby. There was tough work in the making of this tunnel, but the most spectacular engineering is to be seen further on.

The line is carried in cuttings through the wild, tumbled undercliff region of the Warren until the huge mass of Abbots Cliff rises ahead; through this Cubitt drove a long tunnel. Although fairly close to the sea the chalk is very sound, and his judgment in this respect has been well proved by the years; the tunnel is as good as ever today, after 110 years. On emerging from the eastern end of Abbots Cliff

Tunnel the line had to be carried on a ledge cut in the chalk, above which the cliffs rose to a great height. Right in the way was the Round Down Cliff, 375 ft. above high-water mark, the formation of which was, at the most favourable estimate, treacherous. To tunnel would have been hazardous, and the plan Cubitt conceived was so novel, and likely to be so spectacular that he consulted General Pasley before embarking on it. His plan was nothing less than to blow the cliff out of the way in one gigantic blasting operation! General Pasley agreed, and suggested that the services of Lieutenant Hutchinson, R.E., should be requested, as that officer had had a similar experience of firing three big charges simultaneously in removing the wreck of the *Royal George*. Hutchinson was duly consulted. Three shafts were sunk from the top

Abbotscliffe Tunnel, the western approach

Pushing Nature out of the way – the scene after the destruction of the Round Down Cliff

of the cliff, and from each a gallery was run 300 ft. long. Into the foot of each shaft the explosive charges were packed; a 5,500 lb charge in each of the outer shafts, and 7,500 lb. in the central one.

The operation was carried out on 26 January 1843, and a vivid description was published in *The Times:*

At exactly 26 minutes past 2 o'clock a low, faint, indistinct indescribable moaning rumble was heard and immediately afterwards the bottom of the cliff began to belly out, and then almost simultaneously about 500 ft. in breadth of the summit began gradually, but rapidly to sink. There was no roaring explosion no bursting out of fire, no violent and crushing splitting of rocks and comparatively speaking very little smoke, for a proceeding of mighty and irresponsible force it had little or nothing of the appearance of force.

After the debris had been cleared, the embankment on which the railway was to be carried at the base of the cliffs, was protected by a massive concrete sea wall. There was, however, still one more obstruction to be cleared before Dover was attained – the famous bluff known as Shakespeare's Cliff. Cubitt does not seem to have been quite so sure of the chalk here as he was at Abbots Cliff, for whereas in the latter tunnel he used a normal double-line bore, at Shakespeare's Cliff he went to the expense of two separate tunnels at some little distance apart, and built them in the shape of very tall Gothic arches. From Shakespeare's Cliff Tunnel a timber viaduct across the beach completed the remarkable eight miles of railway that began at the western end of the Foord viaduct.

Today electric and diesel hauled trains race over the lines laid by the Stephensons, by Brunel, by Locke and Cubitt, at speeds no more than vaguely foreseen by those great pioneers, and their work has faded from our memories, where once they were household words. Today we expect our engineers to carry us to the moon and beyond; but we should not forget it was Brunel who once said 'I shall not attempt to argue with those who consider any increase in speed unnecessary. The public will always prefer the conveyance which is the most perfect; and speed, within reasonable limits, is a material ingredient in perfection of travelling'. Although we have not yet reached the stage of public transport to the moon (!) it was the heroic achievements of men like Brunel, in laying the railways of the nineteenth century, that set us one giant step on the way.

The later history of the locomotive

J. T. van RIEMSDIJK

The success of the *Rocket* established Robert Stephenson and Company as the leading locomotive builders, not only in Britain, but, of course, in the world. In 1830 there were only two countries overseas where locomotives had actually been built. One was France where Marc Seguin, having imported two Stephenson locomotives of the vertical cylinder and overhead beam type, was building a number of improved versions with multitubular boilers. The other was the United States, where one locomotive had been imported from England in 1829 – the *Stourbridge Lion* built by Foster, Rastrick and Co., and closely similar to the *Agenoria* of the Shutt End Railway, which came from the same builders and is preserved in the railway museum at York – and two small locomotives had been built: Peter Cooper's *Tom Thumb* and E. L. Miller's *Best Friend of Charleston*. It may be said that the early entry of these two countries into the field of locomotive building was symptomatic of things to come, because France and the United States were the only two countries which were eventually to make a major contribution to the later development of the steam locomotive, apart, of course, from Great Britain. Other countries contributed only details.

Between 1830 and 1870 the greater part of the British railway system was built, an enormous passenger traffic unexpectedly revealed itself, speeds rose rapidly, and improved carriages for passengers, together with increased industrial activity requiring the movement of goods, all resulted in a large demand for more, and more powerful, locomotives. As a result, many new locomotive building firms started in business, but with the one exception of Bury, Curtis and Kennedy, they for many years followed the practice of Robert Stephenson and Co.

Stephensons first modified the 'Rocket' type by incorporating the firebox in the boiler shell, in what became known as the 'Northumbrian' type. Next, they moved the cylinders to a forward position in the bottom of the smokebox at the front of the boiler, where they were kept warm and thus produced more power, while initial condensation upon starting was reduced, to the benefit of bystanders who might otherwise be showered. The disadvantage of this arrangement was that the drive had to be onto a cranked axle – a difficult thing to make, and none too dependable at a time when, it must be remembered, there was not yet a steel industry. To safeguard against accidents due to breakage of this vital component, it was carried in four bearings, one on each side of each driving wheel. This necessitated four frames, two inside the wheels, supporting the cylinders and boiler, and two outside, braced to the inner ones where possible. Large iron plates could not be made in the early years, so the framing was of wood, with iron plates attached to carry bearings and other attachments. This type, on four wheels, became the standard engine of the Liverpool and Manchester Railway. The first of them was the *Planet*, which had carrying wheels at the front, and driving wheels at the rear, the crank axle being just ahead of the firebox, which was carried quite deep between the frames to allow a thick fire to be kept below the level of the boiler tubes. The fuel used in all locomotives in the first half of the nineteenth century was coke, because coal produced smoke and also fouled up the boiler tubes.

In 1833, Stephenson's produced a six-wheeled

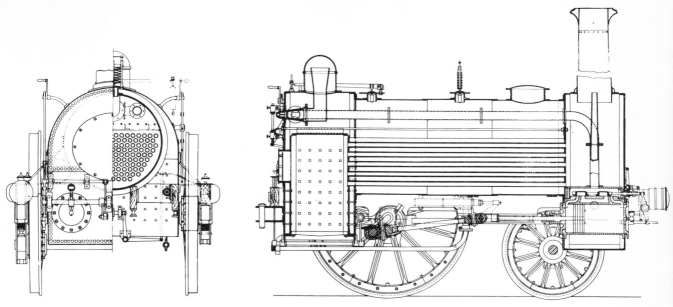

The Planet *locomotive: front and sectional side elevations*

Stephenson's Patent *2-2-2 locomotive*

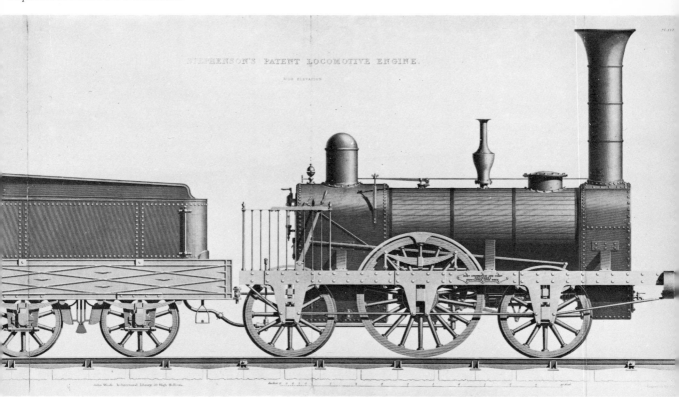

version of this design, with an extra pair of carrying wheels behind the firebox, which made the running steadier. This was known as the 'Patent' locomotive, or sometimes as the 'Patentee', because it was extensively built by other firms, but still bore the words 'Stephenson's Patent' or 'Robt. Stephenson Patentee' on the works plate. There are more locomotives of this type preserved (or reconstructed from the original drawings) than of any other early type, because this was the locomotive that inaugurated so many of Europe's railway systems. The first railway in Germany, from Nuremberg to Fürth, opened in 1835 with a Stephenson Patent Locomotive named *Der Adler*. In the Netherlands Railway Museum in Utrecht stands the reconstructed first locomotive of the Amsterdam Haarlem Railway – a broad gauge version of the Patent locomotive, named *De Arend*. Swindon Museum has a reconstruction of the famous Great Western broad gauge engine *North Star*, which is simply an enlarged version of the same classic type, and the familiar outline is still to be seen in museums in Italy, Denmark and elsewhere. It was not only built in Britain: the great German locomotive building firm of Maffei at Munich began their production in 1841 with an unmistakable Stephenson 'Patentee'.

The chief merits of the design were that it was in keeping with the materials and manufacturing methods available in its time, and that it was capable of considerable enlargement and adaptation without running the risk of encountering unfamiliar difficulties. Thus, for freight service, it was possible to make all the four leading wheels of equal (small) size and couple them, to produce a 0-4-2 type in place of a 2-2-2. Such a locomotive is the *Lion* of the Liverpool and Manchester Railway, the star of the film *The Titfield Thunderbolt*. The coupling necessitated the fixing of small cranks to the ends of the axles outside the outside framing, to take the coupling rods, and eventually these were extended to the rear wheels also, giving the 0-6-0 type which, even in this double framed style derived from the 'Patent' locomotive, lasted into the mid-twentieth century, though with the

benefit of steel axles and with no wood left in the framing. Perhaps the largest examples of this concept were to be found on the Great Western Railway, where Daniel Gooch developed it through several generations of express engines into a celebrated class of 4-2-2 with driving wheels of 8 ft. diameter. The last examples of these, built in the 1880s, weighed over 40 tons and had a grate area (this dimension being a reasonably satisfactory single index of power) of 25 sq. ft., which is just half that of the largest engines ever used on British railways. The large grate area was made possible by the broad gauge of 7 ft., which allowed a wide firebox to be fitted between the wheels, and the general proportions of the boilers of these engines were not commonly found on the standard gauge for another quarter of a century.

On the standard gauge, the Stephenson 'Patent' concept found its greatest exponent in Matthew Kirtley, locomotive engineer of the Midland Railway from 1844 to 1873. It is a sufficient tribute to this designer's greatness to point out that a few of his freight locomotives survived to be taken into British Railways stock in 1948, seventy-five years after his retirement. Kirtley worked on the 'Patent' style of engine all his life, and progressively updated the detail design and improved the materials of construction, as well as enlarging the locomotive to deal with the increasing power requirements of the railway. His last locomotives of the type weighed 36 tons, without their tenders, as against about 15 tons for the original 'Patentee', and had a boiler with 17 sq. ft. of grate, carrying a pressure of 140 lb. per sq. in. These were of the 2-4-0 type, because coupled engines gave better adhesion and the Midland Railway had some formidable gradients on its route over the Pennine Chain between Settle and Carlisle. The 2-4-0 was to be preferred to the 0-4-2, like *Lion*, for passenger locomotives, because it was easier to accommodate large wheels, with their inevitably high axles, at the rear, with the axle behind the firebox, than at the front, where the axle would encroach upon the space required for cylinders and driving mechanism.

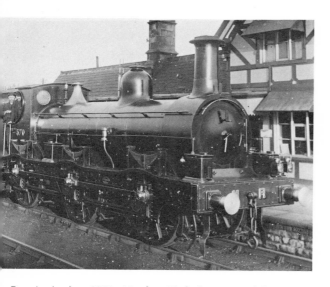

Running in about 1900 – Matthew Kirtley's 0-6-0 goods locomotive type, built for the Midland Railway in 1866

Kirtley built 2-2-2 express engines, 2-4-0 express engines, 0-6-0 goods engines, and also 0-4-4 tank engines for local passenger services. These last, some of which were still working in the London area in the 'thirties, were an unusual variation of the 'Patentee' concept, but really amounted to the *Lion* type, extended at the rear to accommodate a coal bunker upon the engine frame. His last design at length departed from the double framed arrangement. It was a single framed version of the 2-4-0, from which it may be inferred that he finally decided that the crank axle had become, in the 1870s, a sufficiently reliable component.

To revert to Robert Stephenson and Company, in 1841 they introduced an important new type – the 'long boiler' locomotive. The concept was very different from that of the 'Patentee'. The long boiler was arranged with the barrel lying over all three axles, the firebox overhanging at the rear, and the smokebox, with the inside cylinders beneath it, overhanging at the front. The advantage of this was that the tube length could be increased by about 50 per cent and more heat extracted from the flue gases. The celebrated painting by Turner, *Rain, Steam and Speed – Great Western Railway*

shows very clearly the disadvantage of the short boiler tubes on the 'Patentee' type of engine in its early years, because the lower part of the smoke-box is glowing bright red. Even in the twentieth century this phenomenon was known to occur with short tubed engines when worked hard, because the blast of the exhaust steam drew flames right through the tubes and these made that part of the smokebox front opposite the tube ends turn red hot.

Another innovation in the long boiler type was the use of single frames of iron, inside the wheels. It may have been on this account that most long boiler engines were built with outside cylinders, to eliminate the troublesome crank axle which was felt to be unsafe unless supported in four bearings. However, it may also have been to lower the centre of gravity, about which there was at this time a great deal of misplaced concern. Long boiler engines had relatively short wheelbases, and consequently rode roughly at speed. This may have brought forward the centre of gravity question, but the solution of lowering the boiler by putting the cylinders outside (which allowed the boiler to be brought closer to the high axle of the driving wheels, as this had no cranks) brought with it the greater evil of greater overhang at the

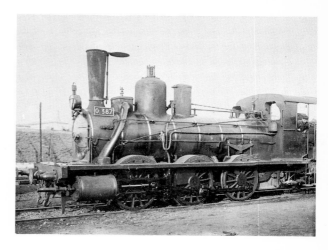

Stephenson's long boiler locomotive, as built for the Eastern Railway of France in the 1870s. The typical European small goods locomotive for a century.

41

front, because the cylinders had to be ahead of the front wheels instead of partly between them. The long boiler engine was not a success in Britain, and the only examples which enjoyed a long life were some large goods engines on the Stockton and Darlington Railway (one of which is preserved in York Railway Museum) which continued working well into the twentieth century, and which had inside cylinders. There were also some outside cylinder goods engines of the type on the Caledonian Railway, which lasted quite well.

However, the Stephenson long boiler locomotive was really a very important and successful design, because it was enormously influential on the continent of Europe. Many thousands of the outside cylinder 0-6-0 version were built, all over Europe, and in fact the European name for the type is, quite unjustly, the 'Bourbonnais'. It was ideal for shunting in confined goods yards, because of the short wheelbase, and this made it particularly useful for long days spent working along the line, picking up and dropping off wagons at every wayside station. From the servicing point of view, the accessibility of the ashpan under the overhanging firebox, and of the outside cylinders – usually with valve motion between the frames in the earlier engines, but not having to share that space with the slide bars, connecting rods and cranks of an inside cylinder engine – made these engines very easy to look after. To this day, examples of the type are to be found at work in Europe.

Enlarged versions of the Stephenson long boiler concept continued to serve continental railways until very recently. An eight-coupled goods engine which was simply an extended 'Bourbonnais' was first built by John Haswell at Vienna, and exhibited in the Paris exhibition of 1855, where it was bought by the French Southern Railway. Haswell was engineer to the Austrian railways, one of the many expatriate British engineers who ran continental railways, and he used the eight-coupled type on the celebrated Semmering incline, but eventually this version of the long boiler concept became the principal European heavy

goods locomotives in the late nineteenth century. In France the 2-4-0 outside cylinder long boiler locomotive was well favoured for passenger service, and when speeds rose to the point where stability became a matter of concern, small trailing wheels were added, giving that form of 2-4-2 express engine which was once so numerous in France, though first built by Stephenson's themselves, to the designs of Robert Sinclair, for the Belgian Luxemburg Railway, in 1860. The long boiler engine was only a failure in the country of its origin.

Yet another concept of the locomotive was due to Thomas Russell Crampton. In this design, the question of the centre of gravity was again to the fore. Crampton's first, and somewhat unpractical patent was taken out in 1842 – the year after the appearance of the long boiler locomotive – but the first Crampton engines were not built until 1846. In order to get the boiler as low as possible, the high axle of the driving wheels was removed from beneath it and placed immediately behind the firebox. This necessitated putting the drive from the cylinders, and the associated valve gearing, outside the wheels. Only the axles of the leading small wheels, and the practical need to provide some depth of firebox and ashpan, limited the depths to which the boiler might sink. The weakness of this layout was, in the short term, that the driving wheels were too remote from the longitudinal centre of gravity and so could not bear heavily enough upon the rails to make the haulage of a heavy train possible. In the long term, the design had no future because the diameter of the boiler could not be much increased without lifting it up clear of the wheels. Crampton in fact used oval boiler barrels in many of the engines.

In spite of the obvious defects, this design was another which, unsuccessful in the country of its origin, enjoyed considerable continental favour. In France especially, long distances and light trains caused 'le Crampton' to enter the language as a synonym for 'le Rapide', and there also one of them, appropriately named *Le Continent*, which was built in Paris in 1852, is preserved in working

A Crampton locomotive of the Eastern Railway of France, photographed in the 1880s

order and has run special trains over some very long distances. The Science Museum in London has a model of a French Crampton, presented to it by Crampton himself, which is possibly the finest locomotive model even in that distinguished collection.

One last pioneer of locomotive design needs to be mentioned before turning to the later part of the nineteenth century. That is the firm of Bury, Curtis, and Kennedy – the one firm which in the early days did not follow the Stephenson lead. Originally the partners were Edward Bury and James Kennedy, and though Bury, having become engineer to the London and Birmingham Railway as well as purveyor of locomotives, is usually credited with the design innovations of the firm, there is reason to think that Kennedy was technically the dominant partner. In 1830 they built a locomotive called *Liverpool*, which was not a success until reboiled in the following year, but it has several claims to distinction. It was almost certainly the first locomotive to have inside cylinders driving onto a cranked axle, so anticipating Stephenson's *Planet*. It was also a long boiler locomotive, though on only four wheels. Finally, it had inside frames only, made of bar, instead of

plate, iron. In this detail it actually followed the *Rocket,* but the framing was much more fully developed, and the firm must be credited with the practical invention of bar framing which was to become the standard practice of American locomotive builders, and to spread elsewhere, right up to the end of steam locomotive construction. Again, this was not a construction favoured on British railways, but its flexibility made it particularly suitable for the engines of the badly laid pioneering railroads of the United States, and in the last years of American steam, cast steel bar framing proved immensely strong and trouble free in locomotives developing the highest powers ever used on rails. Bury himself left the London and Birmingham Railway after some fifteen years, because he persisted in supplying it with his admirable, but undersized, locomotives, and declined to believe that more than four wheels were needed on a railway locomotive. But his design was clearly the basis of that developed by the American pioneer locomotive building firm of Norris, in Philadelphia, which led to the classic American 4-4-0.

In the first half of the nineteenth century the development of the steam locomotive was clearly largely a matter of making the best of available materials, and that state of affairs applied equally to the track, which in its turn limited the designs of locomotive which could run upon it. Alongside this practical necessity there was a good deal of theory, especially at the beginning, but it must be remembered that the science of thermodynamics was in its infancy, and it was not until 1849 that J. P. Joule made an accurate determination of the mechanical equivalent of heat. Generally speaking, it was not until the twentieth century that scientific attitudes began to prevail among locomotive engineers in Britain. On the other hand, the practical and experimental expertise of nineteenth-century engineers ensured that the locomotive became more than just a reliable machine – it became a magnificent achievement, daily under the eye of the public, and frequently noble in aspect. The natural form of the machine was embellished with elaborate paintwork and polished metal, but always in such a way as to emphasise its shape. The Victorian artistic solecisms of putting skirts round the legs of pianos, or building mills in the style of ancient Egyptian temples, were not perpetrated upon locomotives, though something of the kind happened occasionally in the United States.

With the improvement in the quality of iron and invention of processes for large scale making of steel, the use of double framing declined and the wheels became more exposed to view. Cylinders were mostly inside in British locomotives, though a few of the best designers still preferred to avoid the use of a crank axle in the larger engines, and the use of inside cylinders was never very widespread outside this country and eventually ceased altogether where only two cylinders were used. Basically, in fact, the *Rocket* concept won the day. However, there were still a great number of detailed improvements to be made, and the problems of increasing size defeated many designers.

The most important change which came about in the middle of the nineteenth century was the substitution of coal for coke as locomotive fuel. There were many and complicated types of firebox tried out, notably by the elder Beattie on the London and South Western, and by J. Cudworth

on the South Eastern, but the simplest and most effective solution, which has sufficed ever since, was worked out on the Midland Railway under the guidance of Matthew Kirtley. By 1859 he had evolved, with the able assistance of Charles Markham, an arch of firebrick spanning the fire and forcing the gases to circumvent it on their way to the tubes. This brought them close to the door through which fuel was fed to the fire, and this door was contrived to admit some extra air, to supplement that which came up through the fire itself, and ensure complete combustion.

It is not possible in a short chapter to pay tribute to all the great locomotive engineers, even of Great Britain, so attention has to be confined to those who made several important contributions to design. Such a one was William Adams, who invented the locomotive bogie in its proper form. This arrangement, of four small wheels on a subsidiary frame capable of rotation about a vertical axis, had been schemed out by William Chapman about the time that *Puffing Billy* started its career, but its geometry was unsound, and insofar as it was used at all on locomotives, it remained unsound. Adams began his career as a locomotive engineer (he had been a marine engineer before) on the North London Railway, where he found some Stephenson tank locomotives fitted with this primitive type of swivelling truck. He built an enlarged version of these engines, and provided the pivot of the bogie with lateral movement controlled by springs. This corrected the geometry, and gave an astonishing improvement to the riding quality of the locomotive, because it now entered curves without shock, the lateral springs guiding the heavy front part of the engine. It also reduced the shock upon the outer rail. This innovation was made in 1865, in Adams' first design, and a few of these engines were still in existence sixty years later.

His next design moved the cylinders from their inside position, which he had at first copied from the Stephenson engines, to the outside, eliminating the crank axle. A good feature of the Stephenson engines had been the provision of balance beams to equalise the weights carried by the two coupled axles, irrespective of undulations in the track, and Adams made this a feature of his designs, providing, with the bogie pivot, a three point suspension for a 4-4-0 locomotive. He developed this concept most notably in his long series of express engines for the London and South Western Railway, the last of which appeared in 1896 (when Adams was seventy-three). Like all his larger engines, these had outside cylinders, which made them very easy to maintain, and bogies with a longer wheelbase than was used by other designers in this country. This made for even steadier running, and it can be said that Adams was particularly successful in improving the locomotive as a vehicle, and ensuring a harmonious interaction with the track. In fact his work in this respect, as in others, was a contribution to the development of the locomotive everywhere, not just in these islands, and he was probably the last British locomotive engineer of international influence, until days of the Garratt locomotive.

Adams started with tank engines, and during his period as locomotive engineer of the Great Eastern Railway he was also responsible for motive power on the London, Tilbury and Southend Railway. For this line he designed the first 4-4-2 tank engines,

which were outside cylinder engines based on his 4-4-0 concept. They were express engines, though used for every kind of duty and sometimes referred to as 'universal' engines. In them he made the important innovation of increasing the capacity of the water tanks by adding, to the tanks in the customary position on each side of the boiler, a third tank behind the cab, beneath the coal space. This has been the normal practice in all but the smallest tank engines ever since. The original L.T. & S.R. engines appeared in 1880 and eventually totalled 36. An enlarged version on precisely the same lines followed, under the superintendence of T. Whitelegg, of which 12 were built, followed by 18 with larger boilers. In 1905 a further enlargement took place, and of this last version no less than 35 were built by the L.M.S. Railway between 1924 and 1930. This is a sufficient tribute to the excellence which resulted from Adams' careful study of the details of the locomotive.

Although most of the revenue of most railway companies has been earned by freight locomotives travelling at low speeds, technical interest centres very largely on the passenger locomotives, because high speeds require high powers. Towards the end of the nineteenth century most British express engines were still based on the six-wheel concept

The London, Tilbury and Southend Railways
4-4-2 tank locomotive, to William Adam's
original design of 1800, but with altered chimney.
The line of rivets on the bunker shows the top of the rear water
tank. The equalised suspension visible between the driving
wheels, and the outside cylinders, are typical of Adam's designs.

of 'Patentee', in the sense that there was a crank axle (or, in the case of outside cylinder engines, a driven axle) in the middle of the wheelbase, with the firebox behind it and the cylinders and motion ahead of it. Behind the firebox was usually another driving axle coupled to the first one, and at the cylinder end the engine was supported by a carrying axle or a leading bogie. This familiar layout was expanded until the spacing of the coupled axles reached 10 ft., first in Dugald Drummond's T9 class on the L. & S.W.R., to accommodate a large grate between the frames. This figure of 10 ft. was regarded as the maximum permissible with coupling rods – though for no very good reason as it was later exceeded without trouble in Holland and, later still, in Ireland. Further to increase the power of the locomotive might involve proceeding from eight to ten wheels and might also involve raising the grate to pass over a high coupled axle.

Around the turn of the century, the problem of enlarging the classic 4-4-0 locomotive was exercising the minds of many designers, and defeating some of the best of them. A common mistake was to progress to a 4-6-0, with a shallow firebox and, because of the presence of that intrusive rear axle, an ashpan which choked rapidly, blocking the access of air to the grate and reducing its effective area to less than that of the 4-4-0 engines. On the Highland Railway, in Scotland, David Jones had produced a successful 4-6-0 goods locomotive in 1894, but it had small wheels and could not really serve as a model. The solution was found by H. A. Ivatt of the Great Northern Railway, in a 4-4-2. It was quite a small engine, built in 1898, and later given a name – an unusual thing for a Great Northern locomotive – Henry Oakley, after the general manager. This very graceful engine was not really an enlargement of a 4-4-0 at all. It was an enlargement of the famous 4-2-2 locomotives of Patrick Stirling, the 'eight footers', which were hitherto the largest Great Northern express engines.

The Stirling eight footers had outside cylinders, and Ivatt followed suit with Henry Oakley. This made it possible to drive the second pair of coupled wheels from cylinders in the normal position over the bogie, and to combine long connecting rods (which are advantageous as they reduce angularity) with a compact wheelbase, which in turn meant that the rear end could be stretched out a little over the small carrying wheels without producing too long an engine. Thus a long grate could be provided immediately behind the driving, second coupled, axle, and this, with its ashpan, had only to clear the low axle of the carrying wheels.

Twenty one locomotives of the Henry Oakley type were built, and then, from 1902 onwards, Ivatt built 92 of an enlarged class, which though on the same underframe, had greatly enlarged boilers in which the grates were widened to pass right over the tops of the carrying wheels, giving a grate area of 31 sq. ft. The boiler barrel was enlarged in proportion and the result was an engine less graceful than Henry Oakley but of very noble proportions. The Ivatt large 'Atlantics' have become a legend in railway circles for numerous feats of heavy haulage and high speed, especially in their later years when equipped by Ivatt's successor, H. N. (later Sir Nigel) Gresley, with large superheaters. They weighed less than 70 tons, and few locomotives, and none in Britain, have exceeded their power output with so small a weight. The design of boiler, with the wide firebox subsequently used on all the large British tender locomotives of 4-6-2 (Pacific) or 2-6-2 wheel arrangement, was copied by Ivatt from American practice, which may be taken as an indication that by 1900 the tide was turning, and Britain was now learning from those whom once she had taught.

Opposite

Patrick Stirling's eight-foot single driver locomotive No. 5, for the Great Northern Railway, 1873

H. A. Ivatt's first 4-4-2 locomotive for the Great Northern Railway, 1898. It was the first British locomotive to be an effective improvement upon the contemporary eight-wheeled engine

H. N. Gresley's first Pacific locomotive, Great Northern Railway, 1922

The outstanding learner among twentieth-century locomotive engineers was G. J. Churchward of the Great Western. In the first years of the century he equipped the G.W.R. with a collection of standard locomotive types, the main features of which were eventually copied all over the railways of Britain, and very largely enshrined in the standard locomotives produced after nationalisation. The inspiration of his first standard locomotives was American. He did not, like Ivatt, adopt the wide firebox, but he copied an American design of narrow firebox boiler, with a tapered barrel and an oppositely tapered firebox, having a square upper part (the square upper part was already common in Britain, but was first used by a Belgian engineer named Belpaire, after whom it is known). He also adopted the American construction of the front of the engine, with the outside cylinders cast so that they could be bolted together along the engine centre line, and the valves on top, driven by valve gearing between the frames. To the practical American design he added two ingredients of his own: very carefully worked out valve gearing to give the most economical use of steam, and a very high standard of construction, which was uncommon in the United States at the time.

The Northern Railway of France had, in 1899, introduced a class of 4-4-2 express locomotives not unlike *Henry Oakley* in appearance, but entirely different in construction. They were compounds, with four cylinders and a high boiler pressure, the steam being used in high pressure cylinders first and then further expanded in low pressure ones. Their design was the result of collaboration between Alfred de Glehn, of the Alsatian Mechanical Construction company, and Gaston du Bousquet of the Northern Railway – the greatest French locomotive engineer of his age. These locomotives had rapidly become very famous, and they were destined to remain in express service for some forty years in all. They had proved themselves capable of exerting a pull of over three tons at 70 m.p.h. Churchward had set himself the ideal of a pull of two tons at that speed,

The Caerphilly Castle, *Great Western Railway, 1923 – now in the Science Museum*

so he very wisely bought one of the French engines and proceeded to dismantle it. 'Watchmaker's work' was his comment on this intricate and beautiful machine, and he bought two more of a slightly enlarged type.

There could be no question for Churchward, an avowed admirer of American simplicity, of adopting the French design in its entirety. This was perhaps a pity, because the later development of this design in France produced the most economical of all steam locomotive types, and those with the highest power to weight ratio. However, Churchward adopted many features of the French design, and in particular the use of four cylinders, the inside pair driving the leading couple axle and the outside pair driving the second. He did not adopt the compound principle, and all four cylinders used high pressure steam. His first four cylinder engine was the *North Star*, a 4-4-2, subsequently altered into a 4-6-0. The rest of the 'Star' class were all six-coupled from the start. The use of four cylinders was confined, on the Great Western, to the most powerful passenger classes, and after Churchward's retirement his successor, C. B. Collett produced an enlarged version, of which the first was *Caerphilly Castle* built in 1923. This was an outstandingly successful design, perpetuated in new construction for a quarter of a century, and further augmented by conversion of many of the older 'Star' class, including the pioneer engine *North Star*.

When new, *Caerphilly Castle* was exhibited at the Wembley exhibition alongside a perceptibly larger L.N.E.R. locomotive of Gresley's Great Northern 'Pacific' design – the celebrated *Flying Scotsman*. The Great Western engine was labelled as the most powerful in Great Britain – a clear challenge to its larger neighbour which made a trying of conclusions between the two classes at some later date inevitable. When this took place in 1925 it was inconclusive, but as the 4-6-2 *Flying Scotsman*, with 41 sq. ft. of grate, weighed well over 90 tons, and *Caerphilly Castle* with only 29 sq. ft. of grate, weighed just under 80 tons, it was very clear that the Churchward valve arrangements enabled the Great Western engine to get more work out of the steam. There was also the possibility that the higher pressure of the 'Castle' – 225 lb. per sq. in. – inherited from the French compounds, gave it an advantage over the other engine, which only had 180 lb. Suffice it that all the L.N.E.R. 'Pacifics' were eventually endowed with Churchward-type valve arrangements and a much higher boiler pressure. It is good to know that both *Flying Scotsman* and *Caerphilly Castle* are still in existence, the latter in the Science Museum in London.

With these two designs of the early 'twenties, the British express locomotive was practically at its peak. Both types were marginally improved upon, the 'Castles' by the even larger and possibly more handsome 'Kings', and the 'Flying Scotsman' type by the streamlined Gresley 'Pacifics' which set daily standards of high speed running not previously seen in Britain, and one of which, *Mallard*, established the world speed record for steam at 126 m.p.h. – a feat the more remarkable in that this type also proved itself suitable for hauling the heaviest passenger trains ever run in these islands, during the war.

The Gresley 'Pacifics' had three cylinders, and Gresley's successors on the London and North Eastern Railway followed more or less the same principles of design, as did Oliver Bulleid when he left Gresley's staff to become chief mechanical engineer on the Southern Railway, where he produced a brilliant series of 'Pacifics' on similar lines anatomically, though of very different external appearance. The 'Kings' had four cylinders, arranged in the French manner, and this mechanical layout had once been attached to a boiler with a wide firebox, in Churchward's solitary 4-6-2 *The Great Bear*. This splendid machine had proved

The longest non-stop run in the world – London to Edinburgh 393 miles – was operated by Gresley Pacifics from 1928 until it was discontinued with the advent of diesels. Here it is in its final years.

unnecessarily large for its period (it appeared in 1908, the year after the first European 4-6-2 which was a four cylinder compound of the Paris-Orleans Railway). However this marriage of the Great Western mechanism with the Great Northern idea of a locomotive boiler eventually took place on the London Midland, and Scottish Railway in the 'thirties, as a result of the appointment to the L.M.S. of a Great Western man, W. A. Stanier. In spite of their obvious derivations, his largest express locomotives were very much his personal creation, and the last of them were the most powerful class ever to run on British railways in steam days.

One or two concluding points must be made to finish this very brief outline of a very complicated and fascinating story. In the first place, it is worth pointing out that locomotives with more than two cylinders were first produced, in any numbers, as compound, or double expansion, machines. The practical compound locomotive was invented by Anatole Mallet and first appeared in 1876. It had two cylinders, as had very many compounds built right to the present day (in South America). In England, F. W. Webb, the influential engineer of the largest British railway of its day, the London and North Western, started experimenting with compounds very soon after Mallet's success. He used three, and later four cylinders, in a series of extremely poor designs, the ill repute of which went far to prevent the widespread adoption of compounding in this country. In France, the first of the great series of four cylinder compounds appeared in 1886, while the most numerous of all Swiss steam locomotives was a class of 147 three cylinder compound 2-6-0 of which the first was built in 1896.

The first British four cylinder simple, non-compound engine, apart from the odd experimental freak, was a 4-4-0 of the Glasgow and South Western Railway which appeared in 1897, to the design of James Manson, an extremely capable engineer, but a rather inconspicuous figure in railway history because he worked for two small and far from wealthy Scottish companies. This engine ran for twenty-five years before rebuilding

and was the only successful four cylinder simple before the appearance of Churchward's *North Star* in 1906. The three cylinder simple came later in these islands – in 1907. The first examples were some heavy tank engines for shunting on the Great Central Railway, designed by J. G. Robinson, which were followed by some not dissimilar but far more elegant engines for the same purpose on the North Eastern Railway, designed by Wilson Worsdell. The North Eastern thereafter made extensive use of three cylinders in all types of locomotives, and this influenced Gresley on the Great Northern (which was associated with the North Eastern in the 'East Coast Route' to Scotland), who subsequently, when both companies had become constituents of the London and North Eastern, became the greatest exponent of three cylinder propulsion, probably in the world.

Compounding, as already indicated, was not popular in Britain. There was, however, one school of compound design which provided a small but continuing thread in British locomotive history. This began on the Great Eastern Railway, under their engineer T. W. Worsdell, who, on moving to the North Eastern produced a number of brilliant two cylinder compounds, some of which demonstrated a power to weight ratio greater than any contemporary engines. Mechanical difficulties led to their conversion to simple expansion under Worsdell's successor, his brother Wilson Worsdell,

A North Eastern Railway two-cylinder compound 4-2-2 express locomotive, designed by T. W. Worsdell, 1889

but there was under him an exceptionally able chief draughtsman, Walter Smith, who persisted with compound expansion and built three very efficient and long-lived compound express engines for the North Eastern, one of which, a 4-4-0 with three cylinders, served as the prototype for the most numerous class of compound locomotive ever to run in Britain. The first of these were built for the Midland Railway, by Samuel Johnson, a friend of Smith, who collaborated in the design. A first 5 were increased to 45 by the Midland, and renewed construction by the L.M.S. brought the total to 240, built between 1902 and 1932. These were very good engines, notable for smooth riding and great power, for their modest size, in ascending gradients, and they lasted until the last years of steam on British railways. The first engine of the class is now preserved in the National collection.

In the first years of the twentieth century the German engineer W. Schmidt perfected a trouble free system of superheating steam on locomotives. Superheating involves raising the temperature of the steam after it has left the boiler proper, to a higher level than that associated with its pressure when in the boiler. It was already a practice used with stationary engines, where it produced important economies of fuel as well as an increase in power. Superheating was difficult in a locomotive, because of strains put upon the pipe system by the movement of the engine along the rails, and because of the very high furnace temperatures intermittently reached when working hard. Schmidt's solution to the problem was a piece of very careful detailed designing, and was the major German contribution to the development of the steam locomotive. It had a very great influence in Britain, as elsewhere, and the man most responsible for its widespread adoption here was D. E. Marsh of the London, Brighton and South Coast Railway, who, in 1908, fitted superheaters to some large 4-4-2 tank engines used for Pullman expresses, among other duties. Of all locomotive details, the superheater is the one which above all deserves to be ranked as a major step forward.

At the end of a story in which all too few of the protagonists have received a sufficient mention, one must pay tribute to them all for producing a magnificently simple and effective machine, low in cost, reliable, versatile, and uniquely suitable for providing the wide fluctuations of power required for working trains. Perhaps the steam locomotive was the one product of the industrial age which, while plainly a machine and nothing more, yet possessed an element of beauty, nobility and drama which evoked a response in a large number of ordinary men and women of the travelling public. Why, one must ask with regret, is it now so nearly a thing of the past?

In spite of a great deal of alleged statistics, nobody has yet been able to prove that there is any more economical way of running a railway than with steam locomotives. The isolation of costs is well-nigh impossible, and new forms of motive power are usually associated with other changes designed precisely to extract the economic maximum from the newly invested capital, a necessary measure because electrification is very expensive, and diesel-electric locomotives many times more costly, per unit of horsepower, than steam ones. All the same, there are a number of factors apart from the narrowly economic, and these mostly favour electrification.

There is in the Science Museum the first electric locomotive of the City and South London Railway – the first 'tube' railway – built in 1890. One would not wish to see, still less smell, a steam locomotive

The City and South London Railway electric locomotive, 1890

in the tube, and a diesel would be just as bad. The first practical electric railway was operated by Werner von Siemens at the Berlin Exhibition of 1879. It was only a little line carrying a few spectators, but it demonstrated traction without pollution. The first electric railway in Britain was built by Magnus Volk, engineer to the Brighton Corporation, in 1883 and it still operates along the sea front, though a fantastic extension of it – a sort of section of pier which ran by electricity through the sea itself, the long legs running on rails on the sea bed, had a short life, despite Royal patronage and the attractions of going out to sea without fear of being seasick.

At the turn of the century there was a great growth of electric tramways which took traffic from the railways, and caused some of them to toy with the idea of electric trains on their tracks. At the same time the technology of electric traction advanced as a result of tramway experience. It was above all the Swiss who experimented with main-line electrification and made the greatest progress in it in the earlier part of the twentieth century; steep gradients, long tunnels and hydroelectric power all combining to make it an attractive proposition.

After 1918 electrification spread steadily in Europe, though in England it was only resorted to where there was a heavy commuter traffic to ensure an adequate employment of the costly equipment. After 1945 the London and North Eastern Railway electrified the first section of main-line which was not a commuter route – from Manchester to Sheffield – where there was a heavy freight traffic, steep gradients, and a major tunnel. Now there is the near prospect of electric working the whole way from London to Glasgow, and Britain is up to European standards of operation on the southern part of this route.

On the continent, France, home of the most advanced steam locomotives, is now home of the most advanced electric trains, one of which is claimed to be the fastest in the world, with running speeds of 135 m.p.h. A test train has exceeded 200 m.p.h. on a number of runs, with every detail of its behaviour being monitored by the railway research staff. But it is in Japan, on the Tokaido line, that the greatest daily high speed mileage is being run, with practically every train reaching 125 on the 320 mile run between Tokyo and Osaka. This is not an old line brought up to new standards, but an entirely new railway, built

Magnus Volk's Electric Railway, Brighton 1883

Tokyo to Osaka at 125 m.p.h. on the Tokaido Express

to a larger gauge than the narrow 3′ 6″ of Japan's older railways, and laid out with sweeping curves and moderate gradients, with electronic signalling and train control and every other aid that modern science can contribute in a highly developed country.

What of the diesel? This, like the steam locomotive, is a prime mover, which means that it converts fuel into power, all on the moving locomotive. The electric train does not do this – it is done in a power station, which can do it more economically and more abundantly, and the train simply picks up the power in the most convenient form, electricity, and converts it to mechanical power in a relatively light device, the electric motor. The diesel is like an electric locomotive with a small power station on its back, and one of limited output. So it is inevitably much heavier than an

electric locomotive, and unable to draw upon a power station for some extra power over a short period, to surmount a gradient. This can be done with an electric locomotive at the expense of a rise in the temperature in the motors, so it is limited to ten or fifteen minutes duration, but this is all that is needed on a slightly undulating main line. This extra power cannot be built into the generator of a diesel electric locomotive without an unacceptable increase in weight.

Even a steam locomotive has the ability to produce an extra effort over a short period, higher than it could maintain continuously. It can do this by allowing the water level in the boiler to sink a little, and even by allowing a pressure drop which can be recouped on a following easier stretch of line. But steam and diesel, both being prime movers, are only really suitable for use where the

53

intensity of traffic cannot justify the high capital cost of electrification, and such routes may eventually prove uneconomic as railways.

There is nothing to choose between the power to weight ratio of steam and diesel electric locomotives, though progress continues with the latter and not the former, so comparisons have to be made with care. But the diesel has the great advantage of not requiring a scarce and expensive fuel (as locomotive quality coal has become) and using, on the contrary, a liquid fuel of small bulk easily made available all over the railway system. In steam days there were many heavy coal trains running simply to keep locomotive depots supplied. Also the diesel has not the insatiable thirst for water — thousands of gallons on a long journey — which required expensive installations all over the system in the days of steam (even if they did ultimately irrigate the crops of a large part of rural Britain). But the diesel, like electrification, is for developed countries, where the driver now prefers a comfortable seat and a clean suit to a swaying iron footplate and a roaring coal-fired furnace, and where plenty of highly trained mechanics and a sophisticated industry can minister to its needs. In the poorer countries of the world, diesels, sold as symbols of modernity, rust all too frequently, idle for lack of spares and suitable maintenance staff.

Perhaps the brightest prospect for a real revolution in railway motive power is that offered by the linear electric motor. This new configuration of the familiar induction motor has been developed, under the guidance of Professor Eric Laithwaite, from a way of propelling the shuttles of looms into the first railway propulsion system which is not dependent on adhesion, which draws power from a central power station, and which has absolutely no mechanical link involved in transmitting the tractive force, because this force is magnetic. This comes so close to the ideal solution that it is to be hoped that it will eventually be possible to convert many of the worlds' railways to linear motor traction, and that this British development will eventually prove as significant as any of the earlier advances in railway technology.

There is now little future for the steam horse. But it is still being built where labour is plentiful, skill scarce, and governments realise the need to develop themselves, rather than have development thrust upon them. And in such countries, with some help from European engineers, steam locomotives as fine as any built in Europe or America may yet see out the twentieth century.

Historic accidents

O. S. NOCK

B.Sc., C.Eng., F.I.C.E., F.I.Mech.E., F.I.R.S.E.

The unexpected is always news, especially where the safety of human life is concerned; and that is why no more serious a mishap than a few goods wagons taking a nose-dive down an embankment hits the headlines, while the smooth running of thousands of other trains is taken for granted. But railway accidents have played an absolutely vital part in the building up of the wonderful safety record of our railways today. The lessons that have been learned from them have contributed much to the advancement of railway operating technique. They are still doing so; for there is always the unpredictable to be contended with. But I do not wish to dwell upon modern accidents – serious and costly in life as some of them have been. I want to refer to some accidents that took place in the early days of railways, in those formative years when men were learning by hard experience the hazards that had to be safeguarded against; the likely points of failure in machinery, operating procedure, and of the human element.

It was not a straightforward process of development; improved machinery and more elaborate methods inevitably cost more money. Engineers were not agreed as to the best way of meeting these challenges; and hard-headed managements weighed the costs against the likelihood of such failures occurring again. One particularly ruthless tycoon of the nineteenth century said openly that he would rather have an occasional disaster, and pay the compensation claimed, than commit his company to the expense of putting on improved equipment on the locomotives and carriages of his railway. And all the time the Inspecting Officers of the Board of Trade, who had the responsibility of investigating the causes of every accident in

which death or injury of a passenger occurred, were pressing for improvement. They could not lay down the law; they could only recommend, and it was often a bitter struggle between them and railway managements when improvements were clearly desirable. But some accidents by their very nature, and their effect on public opinion proved to be landmarks on the road to progress. They were not necessarily those that involved the heaviest casualty list, and indeed the worst accident in British railway history, that at Quintinshill, near Gretna, in May 1915, was due solely to the negligence of two signalmen, who were convicted of manslaughter and served lengthy prison sentences. This was fortunately a very exceptional case, because otherwise the hard facts of the majority of accidents are lighted by records of heroism and devotion to duty on the part of operating railwaymen, often struggling to compensate, by their own efforts, the deficiencies in equipment they then had to use.

In the early days of railways there must have been many hair-breadth escapes from disaster through lack of communication, and the lack of a proper system of regulating the traffic. Sometimes however several factors combined to turn the scale, and change a hair-breadth escape into a catastrophe. This was the case on 9 June 1865 on the South Eastern Railway, when the 'Tidal' boat train from Folkestone was wrecked in a most dramatic manner. At that time the harbour at Folkestone used by the cross-Channel Packet Steamers was a very primitive one, in which the ships could berth only at certain states of the tide. Consequently the running times of the boat trains in connection with these steamer services varied every day. Time-

tables were prepared showing the running of the Tidal boat train from Folkestone for every day in the month, and these were issued to stations, signal boxes, and other people concerned with the running of the trains so that they knew when the train was expected; and on this particular day one person vitally concerned was the foreman of a gang of platelayers who were working on the line near Staplehurst.

The regulations concerning repairs to the line were scanty to say the least of it. What happened on that day in June 1865 no doubt led to the imposition of much stricter regulations for track repair work. Near Staplehurst the line crosses a small stream called the Beult on a bridge so low that a traveller of today would hardly realise there was a bridge at all. But in June 1865 this bridge was the precise site of a track repair which involved renewing some of the bridge timbers. With present-day regulations and present-day traffic such a job

as re-sleepering is done only on Sundays. In this early case it involved taking out the rails, and replacing the longitudinal timber baulks by new ones. There were thirty-two of these baulks that had to be replaced, and the bridge foreman and his leading carpenter had been systematically replacing one baulk after another between the passages of trains.

In this earlier stage of railway development the permanent way foreman was permitted, apparently, to decide for himself when to carry out the job, and on the fatal day only one of the baulks remained to be replaced. The whole operation had so far proceeded very smoothly. No mention of it had been made in any working notices, and not the slightest delay to traffic had occurred. That it was a very risky thing to do was not fully appreciated. But worse than this, familiarity with the job led to some slackness in carrying out such safety regulations as were required.

Of course, as men who were working on the line every day of their lives, the foreman and his gang knew all about the Tidal boat train and its variation in times from day to day; but on the very last day, when one more baulk replaced would have seen the job completed, the foreman unfortunately looked up the wrong date. There was nothing in the system of communication then available that could warn him of the approach of a train, and so after the previous train had gone according to schedule, and the signals he could see from the bridge had been replaced to the 'Clear' position, under the usual 'open block' then operating, he and his men got to work, removed the rails, and set about replacing the timbers beneath. Unfortunately to his initial mistake of reading the wrong day, and so getting a completely wrong idea when the Tidal boat train would be expected, he posted his flagman much nearer to the bridge than the regulations required.

Very soon after they had commenced work and the rails were removed, up came the Tidal boat train at full speed. The driver got the warning from the look-out man, but it was not enough. The man was much too close to the bridge and with the very ineffective brakes then in use there was not a hope of the train being able to stop. The train came to the gap in the rails, crashed down on to the iron girders of the bridge and ploughed its way along. By the greatest of good fortune the engine and the first two carriages got across to the far side and came to rest on the ballast on the firm embankment with one of the carriages still perched in a most precarious position on the end of the bridge. But the couplings broke between the second and third carriages. The impact fractured the cast-iron bridge girder; the third carriage swerved to the left, and once it was detached from the portion of the train still coupled to the engine it was completely devoid of brakes. Everything happened so suddenly that the guard at the rear end had no prior warning and had no time to get any sort of brake force on to the rear end of the train, and five coaches of the detached train went over the bridge and crashed into the swampy fields and the river Beult itself.

The carriages were of flimsy wooden construction; all were four-wheelers, and with the force of the fall they shattered themselves to pieces in the field and in the river itself. In this shocking accident ten persons were killed and forty-nine injured. Dramatic as were the circumstances, the lack of railway operating principles which the accident revealed was even more significant. The fact that a permanent way man could decide entirely on his own when he was going to start taking rails out of a main line on a week-day leaves one in amazement today. No less astonishing to us today is the fact that the regulations then prevailing could permit an express train to come upon such an obstruction as a piece of line removed without the driver being forewarned that any

57

repair operations were in hand. Several more serious accidents were however to be suffered in this country before the danger of the 'open block' and of the time interval system of signalling were eventually condemned.

The dangers of the 'open block' were emphasised in a still more startling manner at Abbots Ripton, on the Great Northern Railway, on 21 January 1876, when two express trains, and a goods train were in collision, and thirteen lives were lost. Weather conditions that night were the worst in living memory. Driving sleet and snow impeded the working of the signalling equipment, and ice formed to a diameter of 3 in. on the wires. Arrangements were made to shunt a southbound goods train, which was running late, out of the way of the *Flying Scotsman* at Holme, seven miles south of Peterborough, but for some reason it failed to stop. The signals at Holme had an arm that worked in a slot in the post; it was not, as is now usual, a counterbalanced unit, but depended for its return effect upon a balance lever at the base of the post. The wire from the signal box to the post had to be pulled, as now, to bring the arm from 'Danger' to the 'Clear' position, and when the signal box lever was put back after the passage of a train the weight of the balance lever brought the arm to danger and also tautened the wire from the signal box. At Holme the signals were working very badly owing to ice having formed on the arms and on the wires.

The station master had instructed platelayers to clear them, and in the subsequent inquiry some of these men admitted seeing several signals wholly or partly failing and sticking in the 'Clear' position. With the method of working then in force, arms stood considerably longer in the 'Clear' than in the 'Danger' position and the mechanism was thus more likely to become frozen at 'Clear'.

On coming to Abbots Ripton the goods train driver, realising that the Scottish express was due, was quite expecting to be stopped and instructed to shunt back into the siding: and although the Abbots Ripton distant signal showed 'White' he thought that the signal might be working badly on account of the weather and slowed down preparing to stop. From his evidence it seemed clear that this distant signal was frozen in the 'Clear' position. The accompanying diagram shows the track layout and signals at Abbots Ripton. Signalman Johnson having been warned from Holme that the goods train had run past all signals was no less aware that his own signals were working badly. He was keeping a sharp look-out, despite the awful weather, and wisely used a red lamp to make doubly sure. The train was duly stopped and instructed to shunt back. In the meantime the *Flying Scotsman* had left Peterborough and was proceeding south under clear signals.

But from Holme onwards, all these signals were showing a false clear, for they were all frozen in the

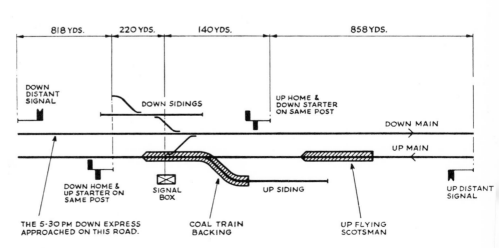

Abbots Ripton. The layout of track and trains just before the first collision

818 YDS.   220 YDS.   140 YDS.   858 YDS.

DOWN DISTANT SIGNAL

DOWN SIDINGS

UP HOME & DOWN STARTER ON SAME POST

DOWN MAIN

UP MAIN

SIGNALS SHOWING FALSE CLEAR:-

UP DISTANT
UP HOME
DOWN DISTANT

DOWN HOME & UP STARTER ON SAME POST

SIGNAL BOX

UP SIDING

UP DISTANT SIGNAL

THE 5·30 PM DOWN EXPRESS APPROACHED ON THIS ROAD.

COAL TRAIN BACKING

UP FLYING SCOTSMAN

The Abbots Ripton disaster, later that night

clear position. The *Flying Scotsman* approached Abbots Ripton at 45 to 50 m.p.h. and came into violent collision with the backing goods train. The signalman, Johnson by name, was thus suddenly confronted with the shock and confusion of a serious accident, and although he was guilty of a fatal forgetfulness, one has to make allowance for the circumstances of the moment. The collision had thrown vehicles and debris on to the down line, but, while realising this and having put his down line signals to 'Danger', he made the fatal omission of not sending the 'Obstruction Danger' signal back to Stukeley signal box two miles to the south, at once. At the moment of the first collision two more expresses were approaching Abbots Ripton, the 5.30 p.m. from Kings Cross, and a Manchester to London train which had left Peterborough fifteen minutes after the *Flying Scotsman*. Signalman Rose, at Woodwalton, two miles to the north, was naturally very much alarmed when the *Scotsman* ran past his box and entered the occupied section. He realized that his signals were showing a false 'Clear' indication, and he acted promptly and effectively enough so far as the up Manchester

express was concerned. The crew of this train saw his red hand-lamp signal in time, and although, like all the other passenger trains concerned, they had no continuous brake, the driver reversing his engine, managed to stop short of the Abbots Ripton distant signal, which they saw showing the fateful white light.

The north-bound express was not so fortunate. When signalman Johnson at Abbots Ripton eventually remembered to send the 'Obstruction Danger' signal back to Stukeley it was received too late by a few seconds; the 5.30 p.m. express was actually passing the signal box as the message came through. There still remained a last line of defence in the Abbots Ripton down distant signal, which, if sighted in time, would have given the driver a chance to pull up. Therein, however, lay the crowning misfortune of the whole affair, for that signal, too, was frozen, and showing a false 'Clear'. The second collision, wherein the 5.30 p.m. down Leeds express crashed into the wreckage of the *Flying Scotsman*, and the goods train, was, however, less severe than it might have been. Immediately the first smash occurred the fireman of the

59

goods train had gone forward with detonators towards Stukeley. He got as far as the down distant signal and fixed his detonators on the down line. He was followed by his own engine, which had been uncoupled from the goods train, and which, in charge of the driver and the goods guard, was going to Huntingdon for assistance.

They had just stopped to pick up the fireman when the Leeds express was heard approaching, and by prolonged whistling and the display of red hand signals, aided, of course, by the explosion of the detonators, they managed to warn Driver Wilson of the express. But he received the warning as he passed the distant signal, instead of a full 200 yards earlier, as he would have done if the signal had been working properly – and that 200 yards was fatal. Apart from the brakes on the tender, all the assistance he had was from the two brake vans on the train. The guards in these vans acted promptly enough in response to his emergency whistle signal, and he himself reversed the engine. But although the speed was thereby reduced considerably it was not enough, and they hit the wreckage of the first collision at a speed estimated at between 10 and 20 m.p.h. In all thirteen persons were killed and twenty-four injured.

The outstanding and fundamental change brought about directly as a result of the accident was in the block working system, which was altered to have the signals normally at 'Danger'. The risk of an arm freezing so as to give a false 'Clear' was thus reduced to a minimum, since the arm would be pulled off only for a short time. If freezing took place in the 'Danger' position, the ice would probably not have had time to consolidate sufficiently to prevent its being broken up when the signalman came to pull off to the 'Clear' position, and in any case if failure did occur it would be on the side of safety. In recommending this change in practice Captain Tyler, the Inspecting Officer, made an important contribution to the safe working of railway traffic.

The other feature of equipment shown by the collision to be wholly inadequate was the braking of the trains. Nevertheless it was the state of the signals rather than the inadequacy of the brakes that received most attention at the time. It was considered that nothing short of double-wire working would have been effective in the very bad weather conditions that existed on the night of 21 January 1876. Apart from that, however, a signal arm that was not counterbalanced in itself was inherently dangerous, and engineers on various railways began to work out new designs. Ideas were not confined to the design offices. On the Great Northern Railway a signal inspector at Hitchin, Edward French by name, proposed the use of a centre-balanced arm, and in September 1877 he took out a provisional patent for it.

In those days the idea of any individual in the service of a railway company taking out a patent for an idea was anathema to the higher management, and French instead of getting any credit for ingenuity got instead a sharp rap over the knuckles. The situation was made so unpleasant that an outsider who was prepared to help French financially withdrew his support, rather than be further involved. Before long French was saddened to see semaphores of the kind he had proposed being adopted as standard on the Great Northern Railway. This is the unhappy origin of the very celebrated 'somersault' arm that became so characteristic a feature of the line for more than fifty years.

At this distance in time it is very difficult to understand why so many of the leading railways of this country put up such a fight against the introduction of continuous automatic brakes. With some administrations one can appreciate that they were looking to the cost of the equipment; but on the contrary some of the largest and richest companies were among the most stubborn in their attitude, while the leading Scottish companies whose finances were not nearly so favourable, were among the first to use continuous automatic brakes. There is no doubt there was much diehard opposition to the pleadings of the Board of Trade inspectorate. One can only conclude that much of that opposition was opposition for its own sake –

a sentiment that refused to be advised by the Government. In the end there was a catastrophe in Ireland, that so shocked public opinion that both Houses of Parliament were ready enough to pass legislation compelling the use of continuous automatic brakes.

On 12 June, 1889, a special excursion train for 800 passengers had been arranged to leave Armagh for Warrenpoint at 10 a.m. A little 2-4-0 engine normally used on the Belfast-Dublin expresses had been provided, but when the load was increased from thirteen to fifteen vehicles, to provide room for all the intending passengers, the driver, McGrath, at first refused to take the train. Immediately after leaving Armagh there is a very heavy gradient, as shown in the profile, but having been taunted by the station master, he eventually agreed to take the increased load. So the train started, at 10.15 a.m. – a quarter of an hour late, with 940 passengers, 600 of them children. As usual then with Sunday-school excursions the carriage doors were locked before starting. Only twenty minutes later the ordinary 10.35 a.m. train was due to leave Armagh on the same line.

The traffic manager, James Elliott, rode on the footplate of the engine, and told in his evidence, that they made a good start; but the statements of various witnesses differed somewhat as to the actual progress up the bank. McGrath said that

once they entered upon the 1 in 82-75 gradient they were losing speed all the way; but both Elliott and the fireman stated that they got on well for the first two miles, after which deceleration began, and led eventually to the engine stalling, ironically enough only 210 yards from the summit. Admittedly the situation was awkward, for there was no hope of restarting on the gradient. Although he was in charge of the train, Elliott consulted McGrath as to what was the best thing to do; and when the driver suggested dividing the train he readily agreed.

This, of course, was the height of folly, for with a Smith brake, vacuum had to be created in order to apply the brake, and any severance of the train pipe put the brakes out of action on that part of the train disconnected from the engine. Matters were made infinitely worse in the Armagh case by the manner in which the train was divided. The intention was to convey the front portion to Hamilton's Bawn, about a mile further on, and stow it in the siding there; this siding was not a long one, and it was believed to be already partly occupied, Elliott gave instructions for the train to be divided between the fifth and sixth coaches from the engine. This meant that the whole weight of ten heavily laden coaches resting on a gradient of 1 in 75, had to be taken by the hand-brake of the rear van. That was bad enough, but on top of it two crowning blunders were committed.

Elliott, in his apparent anxiety to carry on with the minimum of delay, went to the van at the rear of the train and told Guard Henry what he had decided to do; and after ascertaining that the hand-brake was hard on he told the guard to put some stones behind the wheels. Without waiting to see that this was done properly and that the guard was back in his van in charge of the brake, Elliott ran back and told the front guard to uncouple. Before doing so, however, this man put one small stone behind the left-hand leading wheel of the sixth carriage – a totally inadequate precaution, yet one which Elliott admits he did not observe him to make. When the train stopped the couplings were all drawn out to their fullest extent, and the front

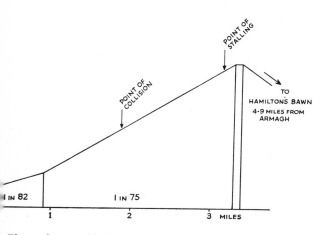

The gradient profile between Armagh and Hamilton's Bawn

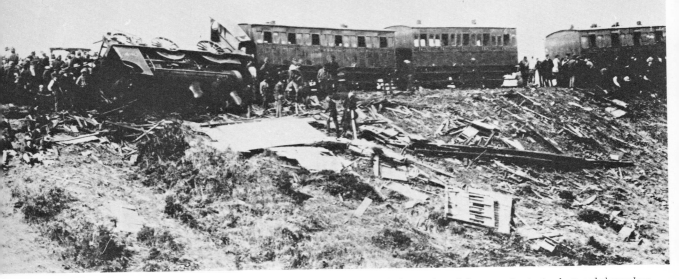

Armagh. The overturned engine of the 10.35 train against which the coaches of the excursion train shattered themselves . . .

guard, Moorhead, seems to have realised, more so than Elliott, that after uncoupling the unbraked carriages of the rear portion would slack back on to the rear van unless scotched in some way.

The actual uncoupling seems to have been done carefully enough, and having observed that both portions of the train remained at rest, Elliott sent Moorhead forward to tell the driver to go ahead, while he himself went toward the rear van. It is easy to be wise after the event, but one would have thought that a railwayman of Elliott's long experience would have been alive to the difficulty, with any substantial load, of making a clean start on a 1 in 75 gradient; there must inevitably be some slight setback between the release of the brakes and the time when the steam began to move the train forward. What exactly happened was not witnessed by anyone interrogated afterwards by Major-General Hutchinson, but Moorhead the front guard, related that he felt his van 'coming back 12 or 18 in.' which he thought was due to the engine setting back. This movement, however, was enough to overcome the one small stone scotching the sixth coach, and the unbraked coaches of the rear portion began to run back. In the meantime Henry, the rear guard, evidently had some difficulty in finding stones suitable for scotching, as he was still out of his van when the runaway began. 'As I was putting down the last stone', he told the Inspecting Officer afterwards, 'I felt the carriages coming back'.

Panic now seized Elliott. Realising at last the peril in which his folly had placed over 600 passengers, he jumped on to the footboard of the rear van, shouting to Henry to get the brake on harder; but then, as the speed increased he jumped off crying 'Oh my God, we will all be killed'. At sometime after the runaway began he seems to have waved the driver back, with the idea of coupling up again, but the front guard, Moorhead, in racing back to try and carry out this measure of despair, fell over some rails that were lying alongside the track, and never got as far as the sixth carriage. The rear part of the train was by this time quite out of control, and accelerating steadily on the steep gradient. The guard, after telling in his evidence of Elliott's last frantic words, said 'The speed then gradually increased, till it became so fast we could not see the hedges as we passed'.

The rear portion of the excursion train began to run back at just about the same time as the regular passenger train left Armagh at 10.39 a.m. That train with its moderate load was making light work of the severe gradient and travelling at between 25 and 30 m.p.h. when the fireman sighted the runaway. Driver Murphy made a full application of the vacuum brake, while his fireman reversed the engine and applied back steam. Although between them they managed to reduce their speed to 5 m.p.h. or less, the carriages of the excursion train were travelling at over 40 m.p.h., and the

62

. . . and fell down the other side of the embankment

results of the violent collision which ensued were appalling. The engine of the 10.35 a.m. train stopped dead, quivered, but did not run back at all before turning over, and against this veritably immovable obstruction the wooden coaches of the excursion train shattered themselves to pieces. Remembering that the train was packed, it does not need much imagination to picture something of the carnage that ensued; there were about 600 passengers, and in those ten coaches 78 were killed and about 250 injured.

Public opinion was deeply shocked. Quite apart from the conduct of the various men responsible for the working of the excursion train, the inadequacy of the non-automatic vacuum brake was clearly revealed. It was also probable that the results of the runaway might have been less severe had the block system been in operation, and the 10.35 a.m. train held at Armagh. Very soon after this accident the Regulation of Railways Act, 1889, was passed, which gave power to the Board of Trade to order the adoption of the space-interval block system, the provision of interlocking, and the fitting of automatic continuous brakes on all passenger-carrying lines. It should, however, be added that most railways, even before the passage of the Act, had progressed some way towards the installation of these three great safeguards, and the fact that such negligence as Elliott displayed took place on a line still outside the pale only deepens the tragedy of the Armagh collision.

There is a close analogy between the change in signalling practice made after the Abbots Ripton collision and the compulsory abandonment of non-automatic continuous brakes decreed by the Act of 1889, resulting from the disaster near Armagh; as the block signals, hitherto normally at clear, were afterwards changed to be normally at danger, so with the automatic continuous brakes, any failure, such as leakage or severance of the train pipe, resulted in the brakes being applied. Work had to be done either to lower a signal or to release the train brakes. With the Act of 1889 the fundamental principles of present-day railway operating were attained, and subsequent technical developments have tended towards elimination of mistakes arising from the human element rather than the establishment of new principles. Although above all a great tragedy, the collision at Armagh, proved later to be a momentous turning-point in British railway history.

By the first decade of the twentieth century British railway operating had reached standards of safety that were the envy of the whole world. It was the Golden Age of railways in Great Britain. Traffic was booming: road transport was hardly a competitor at all – let alone a serious one – and there is no doubt that individual railwaymen were kept very busy, especially at peak holiday periods. As always hitherto, the safety of working largely devolved upon two groups of men, the signalmen, and the locomotive drivers and firemen.

Accidents from this time onwards tended to arise from failures of the human element, which could usually be traced to some extraordinary circumstances; and this was no more vividly the case than the events leading to the disaster near Hawes Junction in the early hours of Christmas Eve, 1910. The Midland was one of the most highly organised railways in the Kingdom. Its express train service was a model of punctuality and comfort; the revenue from its goods and mineral traffic was princely; and yet its methods were such that an act of simple forgetfulness on the part of a steady and painstaking man of humble grade was to lead to an accident that brought odium upon the company out of all proportion to the magnitude of the occurrence or of the death roll. Yet if the circumstances that led to that mistake are traced back to their basic origin they take us far away from any details of signalling at Hawes Junction, and lead to matters of high managerial policy, and the clash of personalities in high places.

During the night of 23-24 December, traffic over the line to and from Scotland was heavy. In addition to the ordinary trains there were many specials, and the majority of them required to be double-headed. Because of the curious locomotive policy of the Midland Railway at that time there were no engines on the system permitted to haul a load of more than 230 tons between Hellifield and Carlisle in express passenger service, and only ten of this largest class, the '999' series, were in regular use north of Leeds. The mainstay of the traffic were the No. 2 class 4-4-0s, which were limited to a maximum load of 180 tons over the mountain section. To save engine mileage the pilots, whether working from Carlisle, Leeds or Hellifield, were detached at Aisgill summit whence they travelled the three miles southward to Hawes Junction, to turn before proceeding light to their home stations. Thus, with the pilots of both down and up expresses coming from Aisgill there was always a number of light engine movements going on in the neighbourhood of Hawes Junction at intervals during the day and night. The accompanying sketch map shows the area.

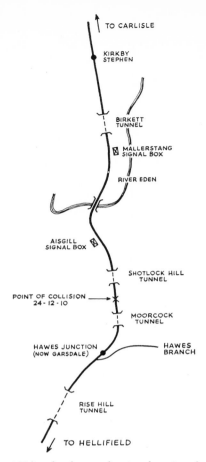

Hawes, 1910 – sketch map showing the point of collision

In the early hours of Christmas Eve, 1910, so many light engines congregated at Hawes Junction as to suggest that almost every train had been assisted up to Aisgill summit.

Around 5 a.m. the Hawes Junction signalman, Alfred Sutton, had no less than nine engines under his control. He was naturally anxious to return these to their various home stations as soon as possible, although the pressure of traffic was still great. An up class 'A' goods train, accepted under the warning arrangement, was approaching from Aisgill and a most important train, the midnight sleeping car express from St Pancras to Glasgow was due shortly. After the passage at 5.20 a.m. of a down special express, Sutton crossed two Carlisle engines, the 4-4-0s 448 and 548, on to the down main line, and these engines drew up some considerable distance short of the advance starting signal. It was the signalman's intention to send the two Carlisle engines away as soon as he received the clearing signal from Aisgill for the special express; but it just happened that when the signal came through Sutton was very busy with other matters. Three further engines were ready to depart, southward this time; the up class 'A' goods was at hand; one of the Leeds pilot enginemen required a message concerning his relief to be sent off, and there came too a telephone inquiry about some Hellifield engines which were at that time on the turntable road.

It will be appreciated that Signalman Sutton's attention was almost entirely taken up with the various light engines and their movements, and in his preoccupation he forgot the two Carlisle pilots. The enginemen of these two locomotives were expecting to be signalled away as soon as the special express had cleared Aisgill, and not one of the four men on engines 448 and 548 seems to have realised that they were being held much longer than would ordinarily have been necessary. Under Rule 55 one of the firemen should have been sent back to the signal box to remind the signalman of their presence after they had been detained for five minutes; but this was not done, and neither driver whistled nor did anything to attract the signalman's attention.

Hawes – burnt out carriages of the Scotch Express

The latter continued to be very busy, so much so that the two Carlisle engines passed out of his mind, and when at 5.39 a.m. he was offered the midnight express from Dent he accepted it at once, and shortly afterwards offered it forward to Aisgill. It was accepted at once by the latter box, so that when the 'Train Entering Section' signal was received from Dent, Sutton merely acknowledged it, all the necessary signals having been lowered when the train was accepted by Aisgill. Of course the light engines 448 and 548 had started away when the advanced starting signal was pulled off about 5.43 a.m., but as the express passed through Hawes Junction at 5.47 a.m. travelling at 60-65 m.p.h. the Carlisle engines had very little start. In other circumstances their tail light might have been seen, but there was a heavy gale blowing, with driving mist and rain, added to which a short tunnel impeded the view ahead.

It was significant of the number of engine movements proceeding at Hawes Junction that it was not until one of the Hellifield drivers came into the box, about 5.58 a.m., and reminded him that Sutton realised that he had forgotten about the Carlisle engines, and that after an interval of eight minutes he had not received the 'Out of Section' signal from Aisgill for the midnight express. When the day signalman came on duty at 6 a.m. there was already a reflection of light on the low clouds driving over the fells north of Hawes Junction. That glow told its own tale, and Sutton said to the relief man: 'Will you go to Stationmaster Bunce and say that I am afraid I have wrecked the Scotch express?' That express, also double-headed, had overtaken the light engines at a point about $1\frac{1}{2}$ miles north of Hawes Junction, and as the speeds were approximately 30 m.p.h. and 65 m.p.h. the resulting collision was violent; even so, the effects would have not been very serious but for a disastrous outbreak of fire. Both locomotives of the express and seven out of the eight coaches were derailed; the first two coaches were telescoped and it was in these that all the fatal casualties occurred. One of the most distressing features of the accident was that some of the twelve persons who lost their lives were still conscious when the fire reached them; the gallant attempts at rescue by their fellow-passengers failed for want of suitable tools, and through the rapid spreading of the fire.

Although the immediate cause of the accident was the simple act of forgetfulness by Signalman Sutton, in letting the light engines Nos. 548 and 448 pass from his mind, it was the plain fact that he had so many light engines to deal with, in addition to the handling of ordinary traffic, that undoubtedly led to his lapse. The enquiry was conducted by Lieut. Col. Sir John Pringle and some of his recommendations were acted upon in so comprehensive a manner by the Midland Railway as to influence subsequent practice in a way out of all proportion to the magnitude of the actual disaster, serious though it was. He recommended track circuiting.

This very simple, but fundamental principle can be explained by reference to the diagram. The line is divided into sections, which are insulated from each other. There is a battery, or other source of electrical power, at one end, and a device called a relay at the other. If there is no vehicle or train on the line, current passes from the positive side of the battery, down one rail, through the relay, and back to the negative side of the battery. The relay is what is termed 'energised', and contacts are made that permit the signal at the entrance to the section to be cleared. But if the line is occupied current from the battery passes through the wheels and axles of the occupying vehicle and cannot reach the relay. The appropriate contacts for permitting clearance of the signal are not made, and the occupying train or vehicle is protected. On the Midland Railway Col. Pringle's suggestion was carried out not only at Hawes Junction, but at over 900 other places on the line, and today the track circuit, in its various sophisticated forms, is the heart and soul of all modern signalling – all over the world.

So, the lessons learned from these accidents – Staplehurst, Abbots Ripton, Armagh and Hawes Junction – have made a major contribution to the safety of railway travel, and perhaps we may feel that the grievous loss of life incurred in all of them was not entirely in vain.

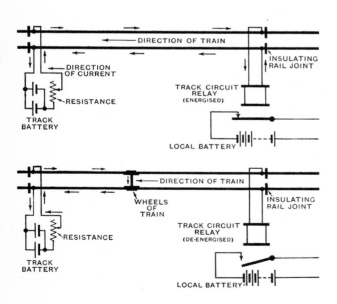

The principle of track circuiting

Corporate images

HAMILTON ELLIS

In this country since 1948, we have had a single, unified, national railway system. While it has contracted under electric or diesel traction its equipment has reached extremes of standardisation. Economically sound, maybe, but meaning for many of us a sort of dull-blue uniformity, which bright-yellow noses to the trains do not relieve.

Before 1948, yet since 1923, Great Britain had four big railway companies. We called them the Groups, for groups they were, geographically and in some Parliamentary wording. There was the Great Western, with lovely green, brassy engines and cream-coloured carriages, fanning out to the West as its name (much older) suggests. There was the largest British railway, the London Midland and Scottish, extending from Thames to Pentland Firth. Its trains were red, and so were the express engines. Then there was the London and North Eastern on the East Coast, but paradoxically going farthest west of the lot, in Scotland, with engines ranging from pea green to garter blue and many black ones as well. Then there was the Southern; compact system – Cornwall to Kent and with its steamers to France, with all-green trains. To those fond of railways, they were lovely!

Now *before* 1923, there were scores, even a hundred-and-more, of British railway companies. Already combined had been the South Eastern and the London Chatham and Dover. The London and North Western claimed to be the Premier Line. Grandly provincial was the North Eastern. The London and South Western and the Great Western (then the largest British railway) faced each other in anger on each flank. Deep south was the London, Brighton and South Coast, at war with both its neighbours, as were many others up and down the country – some great; some small but with immense traffic, like the Taff Vale, and some of the smaller ones were among the best, like the North Stafford and the Great North of Scotland. Among the very smallest there was the Festiniog (which is still there, and independent at that!).

It was the same in Scotland; the Great North of Scotland Railway at Aberdeen always wanted to reach Inverness, which the Highland Railway at Inverness would prevent at any cost, however bare the bank balance. To the last, which means 1948, there were a sort of frontier posts at Elgin and Keith, though for about half a century sanity had prevailed to the extent of joint through trains.

All these variously allied and hostile railway companies had very marked individualities, outwardly shown in appearances, even to variously genuine and spurious heraldic achievements. The Great Central Railway had quite a genuine one with *locomotive engine proper* for its crest. The Caledonian simply bagged the Scottish Royal Arms, and the London and North Western as simply reversed the figure of Britannia from the coins of the Realm. But the Great Eastern embraced within an heraldic garter the arms of every city or town it served or hoped to serve; making a metal casting, having that painted in splendidly correct heraldic colours by skilful Railway Servants' Orphanage girls, and mounting such castings on its superior express engines. It made a lovely object! When it got grubby it could be quickly swapped for a new one, keeping those virtuous girls fully occupied.

Today one may ask *how on earth* did all this variety start, with all these different railways much in competition? How? Only with maps can one understand. Consider a map of England, Wales and Scotland, without any railways. (Don't forget that we had an ever-ready sea coast which, with primitive pre-Macadam roads, had served us from remote time.) On such a map you can mark where the coal was, where the iron was (and in the West, where the china-clay, tin and alleged gold were). Heavy minerals were the cause of the first railways, which were all tied up with coal and iron, especially coal, and with getting the stuff down to wharf or staithes on some river. Starting from the year 1825, we can draw in the Stockton and Darlington Railway, built to bring coal down to Tees shipping. The line was very short. Coal went by steam; passengers had horse-traction in between the terrible locomotives. Five years later there comes the first inter-city line, between Liverpool and Manchester. This was quite a respectable railway. It had up and down roads, with proper stations, signals of a sort, and all traffic by steam traction. Before the end of the 1830s we have Robert Stephenson's London and Birmingham line, and Joseph Locke has built on with the Grand Junction Railway, linking this with the Liverpool and Manchester at a Y-junction near Newton-le-Willows. *That* gives us the beginning of a national trunk railway system, which is one reason why the London and North Western was to call itself The Premier Line a little later, when it had 'taken-over'.

So came other inter-city lines, and people, having seen that the earliest of them were prosperous as well as workable, became very excited at the prospect of getting rich quick. The first boom was soon to be succeeded by one so extravagant that it was called 'The Railway Mania'. The editor of *Punch* produced an extraordinarily prophetic railway map. It was intended to be a gross exaggeration. It even showed railways on the Isle of Man, which was regarded as absurd, but in fact that did happen, and there is still a steam one there. (Not yet, however, is there a floating line across the Channel!)

But this sort of thing *did* happen. There were many phoney undertakings, and chief of the great

The railway age – Punch's 1845 vision of the future

speculators was, of course, George Hudson. He had joined, and married into, a draper's establishment in York. (The building is still there; now a sweet-shop.) Hudson made an immense amount of money, though his business methods were deplorable, and the ultimate examination of books was rather curious. He was made Lord Mayor of York. Then of course, the whole bubble burst. *The Times* helped with a pair of pungent leading articles. There was a great deal of distress. Respectable parties destroyed themselves. Widows and orphans were in the gutter. Hudson ultimately retired to France on an annuity of £500 a year, subscribed by friends, and the affair even had its reflection in literature of the period, from Tennyson's *Maud* to Trollope's novels. But at the same time, Hudson and his kind did cause a number of very good lines to be built. The *Punch* map was not so absurd as it had seemed at the time. A Railway Clearing House map of the industry in its prime is not at all unlike it apart from the Outer Hebrides and some other places.

Of course this meant a considerable amount of duplication through business rivalry. Take the old

Liverpool-Manchester business. Ultimately there were three main-line railway routes between these two cities. There was the Lancashire and Yorkshire company's route north by Wigan and a southern one belonging to the jointly-owned Cheshire Lines, with the original (owned by the London and North Western) between them. On a grander scale there came to be three main routes between London and the North, including the Scottish cities. There was the West Coast Route, passing between Liverpool and Manchester to the Border by Carlisle. There was the East Coast Route by York, Newcastle and Berwick. Then from 1876 there was the Midland Route which, apart from also looking in at Carlisle, had nothing to do with the West Coast. Both East Coast and Midland (after 1868) joined London and Leeds. All three routes got into Edinburgh, and into Glasgow, with no common ground except briefly at Carlisle and outside Edinburgh.

With three routes already between Manchester and London, there came, at the turn of the century,

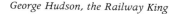

George Hudson, the Railway King

a fourth. For years there had been a Manchester, Sheffield and Lincolnshire Railway. In the 1890s it renamed itself the Great Central, by virtue of a brand-new branch line to London via Nottingham and Leicester, and, far south, Aylesbury, whence concurrence with the London Metropolitan Railway helped a lot. In London this G.C.R. built a most grandiose terminus at Marylebone, the last of the London terminal stations. Whatever the business wisdom behind it, this was a lovely railway. It went through some of the best of England; also it had, in and out of Marylebone, some beautiful trains, including what was the fastest out of London when I was a boy – the *Sheffield Flyer*.

It was the last to be born and the first of the great main lines to die. Where railways die, you can still see their formation, as you can still see the mark of Hadrian's Wall and other, even older remains, across the country. The routes of the dead railways may return, in one form or another, for they can support heavy land traffic with much less space than on a motorway.

But, as to this Great Central; even in its earlier days it was not entirely happy. When it was still the Manchester, Sheffield and Lincolnshire, its initials gave it the nickname of 'Money Sunk and Lost', and as the Great Central it became the 'Gone Completely'. That's an old chestnut, and there were many others. The original Great Western main line wandered about a bit, so G.W.R. automatically became the 'Great Way Round'. And an appendage of that was the Oxford, Worcester and Wolverhampton Railway, which of course – and quickly – became the 'Old Worse and Worse'.

As you may guess, there was plenty of rivalry between the old railway companies. Some was good, some bad. Sometimes it led to bloodshed. Let us go south for an example. In the late 1850s there was a great quarrel between the London, Brighton and South Coast Railway and the London and South Western over running powers which the latter had acquired into Portsmouth via Havant. These, over a line built by a private contractor, gave the South Western company a shorter route into Old Pompey. The Brighton company greatly disapproved and there was a terrific battle between the irregular forces – and police – of both companies on the junction at Havant. The South Western captured a Brighton locomotive which had been padlocked to the junction, but was later forced to withdraw. The lawyers alone won that battle, while the companies settled down to a rate war, likely to beggar them both until they ultimately reached – thanks again to the lawyers – a working agreement.

Such things went on, in Lancashire and in the West Midlands as well as in the South. People were inconvenienced and annoyed, and they also said that rivalry of this kind led to accidents. It may have done so, once or twice. Even in the early part of this century, there was great rivalry between the Great Western and the London and South Western companies (old enemies) for the West of England, especially the then heavy American traffic via Plymouth. In 1906 the Great Western completed a new cut-off, making its own route shorter. On the same day (1 July) after the rival boat trains had been racing each other through the night for some time past, the South Western's flyer, full of Americans, went far too fast round the reverse curves at Salisbury and smashed itself to atoms. We shall never know *just* why. The abstemious and highly respectable South Western driver, with his fireman, died instantly – as did half the train's company.

There were jollier results of such rivalry, however. There had been the great *Races to Aberdeen* back in 1895. There had been betting on rival trains. At Dover, by the old Lord Warden Hotel, people used to wager on first-arrival of either the South Eastern or the London, Chatham and Dover with their intentionally simultaneous Continental expresses. These were quite out of sight of one another until the last minute, when with luck the 'Chatham's' train might come slinking in first from Dover Priory. The present electric trains (which do not race each other) may be much more convenient and 'civilised', but with the old (and sometimes elegant) steam rivals, there was a real sporting event. And one night – dark and bleak –

The Battle of Havant – *a modern artist's impression*

the rival conductors, who were brothers, had a most unfraternal fight for possession of a single passenger for one of the rival 'Club Trains' (subject to Wagons-Lits supplement and therefore shunned by thrifty Anglo-Saxons).

Now apart from such sport, what were the old company-owned railways – the real old ones – really like? The answer is that they were all different from each other, in either stations or trains, not to mention tracks. As to that last, a passenger in the best of sleepers could tell when he was north of Carlisle – Caledonian instead of London and North Western – though he remained in the same bed on the same train. The North Western gave you a gentle *duddididun,* at its highest speeds. The Caledonian gave you a *racketty-tacketty* which was less gentle.

Let us come back to the south. In London, there are still two obviously different Victoria Stations. The London, Chatham and Dover (with interested support from the Great Western) had put up quite an imposing terminus while the London, Brighton and South Coast had an awful set of barns, ultimately, in the early 1900s, replaced by the superbly post-Victorian station we still know. Nowadays the Chatham Side is the poor relation! The South Eastern had a very impressive terminus at Cannon Street, a most distinguished building largely destroyed by bombing in World War II, and another at Charing Cross, the handsome old roof of which fell down much earlier. Of Cannon Street, the two splendid towers facing the river are about all that is left of the old place. But Kings Cross on the Great Northern, and Paddington on the Great Western, though also severely treated by war, remain just as they always were in all important architectural features. Paddington, indeed, remains a real beauty, though nowadays both stations are sullied by the stench of diesel exhaust. That, by the way, is something that particularly afflicts Edinburgh Waverley Station, which is now the city's only big terminal. It became the second largest one in Great Britain, and long ago had compelled on it a relatively low, flat roofing which supposedly saved the view and spoiled the then steam-laden atmosphere. In Scots Law the governing factor was called *servitudes,* which in the southern vernacular are called *ancient lights.*

Euston Station in London was one of the most meritorious – architecturally – in Europe, but as a railway station it was extraordinarily inconvenient and difficult to work. Its successor – as a railway station – is admirable, and for Classic-Grecian one may still turn to Huddersfield, which has been considerably cleaned up lately. The best and most skilful transformation of an old terminus to a modern terminal (note the two terminologies!) has been that of the Gare de l'Est in Paris. In London, the transformation of Waterloo from a fearsome set of old iron and wooden hangars to a very convenient railway station was, from an artist's point of view, less happily carried out. In my infancy the place had – among all the others – a single line, with a level crossing in the middle of the station, to connect the South Western with the South Eastern. The companies were generally on good terms. Sometimes a horsebox or two, or a hired family saloon, would be worked from one to the other. Of the two railways, the South Western had its stodgy goodness as to trains. Its best was

generally inferior to the Great Western's best. Its worst was much superior to the Great Western's worst. The South Eastern was a *showy* line, but its trains were more than ordinarily grim if one travelled in its third class. It was entirely possible to love all three.

The same intense rivalries could be seen among all the other railways in Britain and in Ireland, full of warring factions. Though the Midland Railway (of England) might have taken over the Belfast and Northern Counties Railway, to an Irishman 'Midland' meant the Midland Great Western, which went from Dublin to Galway and elsewhere and had nothing to do with either the Great Southern and Western (a bigger line which went to Cork and many other places), or the Great Northern (Ireland) which, again, had nothing to do with the establishment at Kings Cross, London. One has already noted the curious 'Common Market' ultimately worked out between Aberdeen and Inverness. The thing was everywhere in the British Isles. In Great Britain, if there were one thing West Coast and East Coast hated more than one another, it was the Midland, which ran rather slower, but considerably more comfortable passenger express trains between the South and Scotland, than they did. When it came to freight and minerals, it was simply what a later generation was to call a rat-race, without fancy trimmings.

Of course, several of the companies had their monopolies, or their near-monopolies, and these had their points. The North Eastern had a practical monopoly of East Yorkshire, Durham and Northumberland. It was a very good railway in its clients' experience. Long ago, the South Eastern, and the Chatham, had tried to divide Kent. The results were dire! There were regional differences. Both Great Western and South Western benefited their passengers by burning good South Wales steam-coal in their engines, while both Kent coal and South Yorkshire coal gave some other companies' passengers a less fragrant and certainly grubbier accompaniment to their journeys. Going north out of London from adjacent termini, one found different *smells* in Cubitt's austere Kings

Cross and Gilbert Scott's flamboyant St Pancras, products of the different coals from South Yorkshire and from the D. H. Lawrence country about Nottingham, though the horrible reek of oil gas for lighting the older trains, and for cooking on most, was common to both. 'Gassing', as far as possible, was done elsewhere, to be sure, but not always!

Early in this century, lovely coloured postcards were made of many British railway stations, as of our best trains, and they convey the old scene now as faithfully as ever they did. One recalls particularly Raphael Tuck's beautiful *London Bridge* (not in fact, a nice station!) and F. Moore's *Express leaving Edinburgh,* but there were many, some of great merit.

As to the trains themselves, they had gorgeous variety, and this was no mere matter of the different colours the companies used in painting them. Nothing else on earth could be mistaken for a Great Western train. There were only remote resemblances – through the migration of Swindon men – in the locomotives of, first, the Egyptian Government (as to design) and the Netherlands Railways (as in combinations of black, green and polished brass). Nothing else (except, again, as to colours) resembled the London, Brighton and South Coast Railway sixty years ago. The Dutch Central copied the livery, which was very elaborate in orange-ochre, but its engines were variously Scottish and German, in other respects unlike anything that ever came out of Brighton. There was a marked resemblance, outwardly, between the Great Northern from London to Yorkshire and the Great Northern from Dublin to Belfast and Derry, but that was because a gifted designer had gone from Doncaster Works to Dundalk Works. Aspect was of infinite variety, and for years now, your writer (who is also a painter) has been happily making retrospective pictures of those lovely old trains. Midland red was quite different from North Stafford red; both were quite different from Canadian Pacfic red, which in its turn was further different from the Tuscan red of coaches on the Pennsylvania Railroad in the United States. Indian red (usually on carriages, but sometimes on engines of the Great Indian Peninsula company) was just that, and different from all the others. Chinese yellow appeared very properly on the Shanghai-Nanking Railway. It was not in the least like Brighton yellow; most of its engines came from Stoke-on-Trent. Nearer-abroad, both the old Holland Railway and the old Italian Mediterranean Railway favoured olive green for engines, but there resemblances ended. In Great Britain the colour range went through all varieties of the three primaries and most of the secondaries (the South Western, long ago, even had one *purple* engine, which was appropriately named *Herod*). Among the majority, either green or black were generally winners.

Now all these variously gay or puritan colours were evidence of company pride and publicity, yet, oddly enough, in the United States where competition was cut-throat (two companies had an unholy smash where they crossed on the level between Philadelphia and Atlantic City!), variety was slight. In Continental Europe, some of the most efficient systems had been built as viable and, at the same time, strategic National services under Government, with no competition nonsense. So it was with Belgium, which nevertheless produced the densest railway network in the world. The French Government parcelled out the country to concessionnaire companies, and told them to get on with their regions and not to poach. Prussia and Russia, each sitting on parts of Poland, soon took strong strategic lines, with either State ownership or pretty strict State control. So it was with a lot of nations, though for many years, British companies made hay in South America. Trains of such near-monopolistic administrations had generally a sombre aspect. *Il faut cultiver ses jardins!* There *was* some brightness. Long ago, Paris-Orleans had all-over brass! Prussian engines had red wheels; Bavarian engines were green; Russian State engines were frequently red under the Tsars (though green under the Soviets); only the Dutch (who for many years had two quite separate major railways) went as gloriously brassy as the

A painting by C. Hamilton Ellis of the locomotive Arundel *heading a Portsmouth train of the London, Brighton and South Coast Railway, and below – the Company's arms*

Arms of the Great Western Railway

*The badges of the Railway Companies
express their individuality*

Great Western and the South Eastern in England. The Belgian engines, to be sure, were *moderately* brassy, but between Holland and Belgium remained an invisible gulf in this, as in other respects.

Which system was better – British free competition subject only to Parliamentary harrassings; unbridled competition, as in the United States; regional concessions, as in France, or in the old Austro-Hungarian Empire, where the royal personages seem to have had several fingers in the various pies; or stern Government ownership with strategic considerations, as in many other countries? (One point to note is that none of these railway authorities were as yet facing the challenge of motors and aircraft.) Where inter-railway competition was most free, the most duplication took place, followed today by the cruellest running-down and killing of once proud lines. That has been bad for such pleasant country as that between Aylesbury, Rugby and Leicester, or between Carlisle and Edinburgh by the old Waverley Route, while Hawick, Melrose and Galashiels without their railway, had otherwise become ghost towns before the motor came!

But whether one be Left, Right or Centre in politics, none but a liar or an ignoramus will deny the extraordinary loyalties, the *esprit de corps,* and the strange jealousies which existed from top to bottom within the old company-owned railways. On our old and wayward friend the London, Brighton and South Coast Railway, in its prime, every driver had *his* engine (which another might drive at his peril if the regular one were sick or otherwise off duty); he had his name painted up in the cab, in very elegant gilt letters, and the mileage run was kept up to date, just below. That seems to have been a convention begun by William Stroudley, the company's locomotive engineer from 1870 to 1889. Outwardly an unromantic-looking little man with peering eyes, about as ugly as Socrates, he was worshipped by his officers, and his rank-and-file, and he produced splendid engines. There were several such locomotive engineers, though no-one would admit that any but his own chief was godlike. Two old

Scotsmen, Patrick Stirling on the Great Northern and Dugald Drummond on the South Western (the latter a most rough and ferocious character) were both thus worshipped as gods in their time, as far at least as the very strict evangelical Christianity of working-class Victorian Britain would allow.

Personages on the Boards, or high up in Traffic and Commercial Departments, were more remote than locomotive men, but one recalls warmly-expressed affection for at least two Chairmen: William Whitelaw (successively of the Highland, the North British and the London and North Eastern) and Colonel Eric Gore-Browne of the Southern. There were Holy Terrors, of course, like Sir Richard Moon, for thirty years Chairman of the London and North Western, and his Chief Mechanical Engineer, Francis Webb. But all London and North Western men would give them unswerving loyalty, especially if there were trouble with such unutterable cads as the Midland company, one of whose trains once rammed a North Western one in Birmingham, though there were many sputters of friction before and after that. It was very like Regimental loyalty. When the North Western and the Midland were among those combined into the London, Midland and Scottish Railway in 1923, things were in some ways difficult for quite a time. It was less awkward in 1948, for the new Regions of the newly-formed British Railways closely approximated to those of the four big companies which had preceded them. The new Scottish and North Eastern Regions were all right too, especially the latter. Anyway, everybody had just spent their emotions in a rather ferocious war, with bombed trains and burnt stations, and they concentrated on resuscitating and running their most famous trains. Very old enginemen still recalled the Chiefs of their boyhood. One remarked that William Stroudley's engines looked just like him from the front; small but thickset, with, on the cab, the same bald, domed forehead and the same peering, owlish spectacles.

We can see survivors of these lovely old engines in museums and on preserved steam lines about the country and elsewhere. Some have even crossed the Atlantic for good. The Canadian Railway Museum at St Constant, Quebec, has both *Dominion of Canada* off the London and North Eastern, and one of Stroudley's from the London, Brighton and South Coast. Bellows Falls, on the border of Vermont and New Hampshire, has two English Southern Railway engines as well as an Irish one and many worthy American pensioners. The French and the Germans have done well for their own veterans, too, not to mention the Hollanders who were among the first to scrap steam entirely.

They are all gone from active business now, and one finds nothing like such variety in the airlines, or in public motor transport. On the old company-owned railways in Britain, there was all the difference in the world even between the various passenger carriages – without the extremes of some foreign lines, for example the Prussian range from red-velvet first-class, to corduroyish second, Spartanly-polished third, and Beotian fourth class). This now elderly user recalls still, with affection, such things as the 'green saladin moquette' in the London and North Western first class, the harsh falling-autumn-leaves plush of the Highland Railway, the ornate branched gasoliers in the older Great Western diners, the remarkable differences between a third-class sleeper from Kings Cross to Aberdeen and one from Paddington to Penzance. Such things are now, from Penzance to Wick, as uniform as they can be. Even the old smells have vanished from the places they belonged to, and that of the North British (by no means disagreeable) was unique.

But, where stations survive at all, some of the splendid Victorian architecture still prevails – I have already mentioned such different excellence as that of Paddington (inside) and that of Huddersfield (outside). But architecture belongs to another chapter.

In the old days and by contemporary standards, some of our railways were good and some were bad. Some went to both extremes. The Great Western was majestic: there is no other word for it, whatever some unspeakable train – all-stations-Oxford-to-Ealing-Broadway-and-then-Paddington – might do on a Sunday morning. That old North Western Premier Line was in fact very variable, though its best expresses were superb. The Midland had lovely trains which, however, it seemed sometimes liable to smash up and burn in bleak places. (It was not *all* bad luck; at one time and another the company worked people very hard!) The Great Eastern offered a sort of shadowy splendour even at Liverpool Street in London, though its commuters could have grim experiences. Praise belongs to the Great North of Scotland, also to the Midland Great Western in Ireland which did its very best with what scarcely could be called a fat living! South Eastern hop-pickers' trains were to be avoided, but there were several good reasons for the awful rolling-stock allowed to passengers whose habits were not always *nice*. There was good and bad, side by side, about the country.

State or company ownership? Well, whichever way you look at it, even admitting that some of the foreign countries mentioned had a more rational approach than we had to planned state railway systems, it can hardly be denied that we – especially when we had 120-odd railway companies linked by an unobtrusive Railway Clearing House – had much more fun!

Comfortable carriage

HAMILTON ELLIS

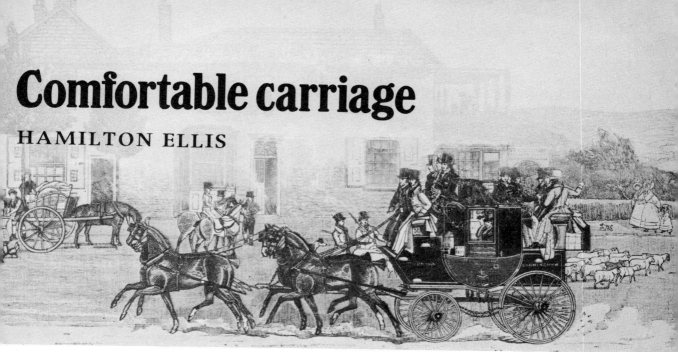

If you are a regular railway traveller, you have a good idea of what you are looking for in a railway carriage. You expect certain amenities; windows certainly, a luggage-rack, lighting, ventilation, sanitation and heating; and, of course, a comfortable seat. Probably you expect some sort of buffet-car or, on longer journeys, a restaurant-car that can serve more ambitious hot meals; breakfast, luncheon, and even a full dinner. Overnight you expect a bed, or even a couchette bunk (though in all overnight conveyance by land, sea or air, people still sit up all night when they must, which is frequently).

In the same way we have all got a fair idea of what the *outside* of the coach should be like. It is made of steel, or of some alloy, or both. Its body is a laterally compressed tube with a semi-elliptical top and a flat bottom. What goes on underneath is none of the passengers' business save in cause of complaint. An ordinary British coach for daytime travel gives either first- or second-class accommodation; or both in a composite coach. In Britain as in most of Europe the first-class is very comfortable and the second quite civilised. German 'firsts' take some beating, while British 'seconds' are much better than most other people's.

The carriage we expect is of steel, then; it is on

well-sprung bogies, and it is lit by electricity, with dynamo and batteries so arranged that the light is constant whether the train goes or stands. It has either a side corridor leading to compartments or else a medial passage. It has flexible gangways to its neighbour-vehicles. It has lavatories easily accessible, and, one hopes, kept cleanly. (One does not expect them in closer city traffic, but sometimes they are there, on many European trains.) One may ask why were such trains, serving the basic human needs, not tried sooner than they were. The answer is that the idea was there a long time ago, in respect of long distances, anyway, but it was never put into effect. That great prophet of mechanical transport, William Bridges Adams, designed such a corridor train – even down to the buffet-car – back in the 1850s. But he, himself, could not risk building a specimen – which would have been awfully expensive, and the railway companies, aiming for quick dividends, would not buy his design. The public, too, was very conservative. It wanted what it was used to, and that was a road coach of some sort, or something very like it, on rails.

Leading in public road conveyance there had been the mail-coach. It was the fastest, most expensive and most exclusive vehicle in use. Next came the stage-coach, which was socially below it, but still very good indeed by the standards of the period. A long way down in quality was the stage-wagon, which was just that – an enormous lumbering freight cart, very slow and carrying passengers on sufferance. But there were, as well, all sorts of private coaches, very elegant and comfortable, though subject to the same hazards as public ones. When the Stockton and Darlington Railway was opened in 1825, it carried its passengers in what was in fact a double-ended stage-coach mounted on railway wheels and drawn by horses (its schedule allowing it to slink along between the steam-hauled coal trains!). People were still rather afraid of engines.

Contemporarily with the coming of steam railways there were steam coaches of various sorts on the roads. They were, however, short-lived because, ironically, the powerful Turnpike Trusts killed them by punitive tolls. I have painted a picture of one built by W. H. James, right at the end of the 1820s. It had a multiple body for inside and outside passengers, with a driver in front and the fireman at the back. From that it was but a short step to the multiple bodies (*compartments* to us) on the Liverpool and Manchester Railway from 1830 onwards and which became a classic first-class form, gradually enlarged and otherwise improved. It is quite obviously a set of three traditional 'glass coaches' (usually privately owned on the roads) combined on one frame, making three compartments, each with six windows. The side buffers were sprung and used with screw couplings, so that vehicles would not bang together in motion or at starting and stopping. At the end of the buffer shank you can just see the buffing spring. The axles are fully sprung as well. At the end of the coach is a high seat for the guard, just as on a stage-coach, and the baggage was all piled on the roof.

This was the most expensive way of travelling by train, but it was considerably cheaper than by the mail-coach, and much faster though, on the basis of first-hand experience of riding in the Transport Museum's replica of the coach, the motion was somewhat violent. But for people in the 1830s, used

to the terrible condition of the roads, it probably seemed quite smooth. Inside each compartment, passengers sat three-in-a-row on divided stuffed seats, which made it rather more roomy than a road coach.

From this it was but a short step to some sort of sleeping arrangement, but such was not for everybody. People were quite used to sitting up all night, or else stopping at inns, so sleeping arrangements were, to begin with, only provided for *personages*, especially Royalty and others who had to keep official appointments. One of the very first 'sleepers' in Europe was built for the Dowager Queen Adelaide in 1842. By then Queen Victoria was on the throne, and old Aunt Adelaide was getting a bit infirm; no longer the lovely young thing familiar to us from her portraits.

The outside of Queen Adelaide's carriage, like the Liverpool and Manchester 'multiple' clearly shows (for it has survived the years) its origin in three road-coach bodies. Notice the continuous footboard below the steps! There was no internal corridor, and it's said that royal rappings were supposed to fetch some intrepid servant along to her, outside the train. One end compartment is like a chariot, probably designed for two servants. In the middle is an ordinary compartment. The other end was the 'bed-carriage', having an extended boot. The interior of this compartment is very interesting. By putting a stretcher with a flat cushion across the footspace, and lifting up a trap-door in the outer partition, a bed could be made up, the Queen-Dowager having both her feet in the boot (the pun is inevitable!). Worth noting, by the way, is the magnificent decorative painting on the outside! Inside, the upholstery was rich and lavish. Lighting was by oil-pot lamps, which were lit outside and then dropped through holes in the roof. Those pot lamps (they were horrors!) are not so far off in history as you might think. They lingered for years in remote places, and your writer last saw them being used for passengers in 1932, at Aberdeen, on a Deeside train.

Since such beautiful coachwork could be made 130 years ago one might have expected that we

A model of the multiple-body railway coach used on the Liverpool and Manchester Railway, 1834

Queen Adelaide's coach, 1842

should come much earlier to the modern railway carriage, or something like it. But no; not a bit of it! For one thing, the Quality did not at all like the idea of 'Common Persons' being given anything so good. So, instead, they got the open second-class, and soon after, the open third-class. Such *common wagons* were just about the bare minimum for moving persons around. They were sturdy enough, built of stout timber, but there was no protection from the elements. They were called 'Stanhopes', a bad-pun euphemism for 'stand-ups'. Eventually it dawned on companies that a few simple planks would allow people to sit down, even though that was discomfort enough. At least, however, these wagons were properly sprung, unlike the coal trucks from which they evolved. Even when a roof was put over the original second-class carriages they were still open at the sides. They were dreadful things! People could freeze to death in them; in fact a Coroner's Jury in about 1840 found that 'the deceased died from cold and exposure while travelling in a second-class carriage of the Great Western Railway'.

But, as suggested, there could be a worse thing than the second class, and soon that was provided, in the phraseology of that same Great Western company, for the conveyance of *the very lowest order of travellers in carriages of an inferior description, at very low speed, possibly at night*. These third-class vehicles at first were simply open, low-sided

goods wagons, with planks laid across, and they were dangerous, too, for people could fall out of them. That happened at Sonning in 1841. A night train ran into a landslip and several of the passengers were killed – they simply fell out and broke their necks.

To understand why these second- and third-class carriages were so awful, you have to understand that, at that time, the upper classes were very much against making it too easy for what they termed *the lower orders* to move about. They were afraid. They felt the threat of insurrection, rebellions and riots! (The ageing Duke of Wellington was particularly anxious. He could cope with Napoleon, but not with an English mob.) Though second-class now became covered-in, more or less, the third-class passengers got little that was better until the young W. E. Gladstone became President of the Board of Trade in 1845 and pushed through an Act obliging all British railway companies to carry third-class passengers at a penny a mile, seated, in weather-proof carriages, once a day, at not less than twelve miles an hour. Further, the carriages, though closed, had to admit light and fresh air. These were the so-called 'Parliamentary' carriages.

While complying with the Statute, the companies ingeniously made the Parliamentary carriages as uncomfortable as possible. They were in fact *vans*. In a specimen on the South Eastern Railway, which for years longer had a bad name in such

'Open air' travel by second class train on the Liverpool and Manchester Railway, 1831

A Parliamentary carriage

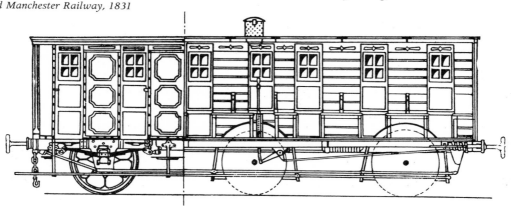

things, there were shutters; you opened them to admit air and light – you closed them to shut out the weather, taking your choice. The Great Western did much the same, though with a larger vehicle, and promoted its third-class unfortunates to a great iron box with tiny windows, and one ridiculous little pot-lamp serving about ninety persons with the guard and his brake screw sitting in their midst. At least he was being paid for it, while they were paying their penny-a-mile which, proportionately to the cost of living then, was more expensive than present-day fares in new pence. (At the time, incidentally, a pint of sherry cost eighteen-pence – old style – in a South Eastern Hotel.)

What is more, the trains ran in the bleak small hours of the morning! One supposes that wretched glimmer helped them in what must have been great bodily distress.

All the same, history was working its way towards the comfort even of the poorer passengers. To start at the top: Queen Victoria had several royal trains built for her, each better than the last by improvement of the carriages. They have not all survived and although there are several pictures of the Royal Family on one or other of their trains, most of them contain a good deal of artists' licence. One, widely circulated, is in fact peculiarly *phoney*. The royal family group is clearly all that matters, with a vaguely sumptuous, totally inaccurate railway carriage drawn about it.

79

The last authentic example of Queen Victoria's special carriages to survive is that built by the London and North Western Railway in 1869, designed by Richard Bore. It was built as two six-wheeled vehicles (connected by bellows) which later were joined together on one long frame. The join in the middle is clearly visible though it was most artistically done. Then the carriage was most carefully sprung, and the twelve wheels themselves had wooden-segment centres, which were long known to give quiet running. The headstocks were furnished with carved lions' heads, gilded, at each end – a delightful sympathetic animal! There was an unusually long set of leather-covered folding steps, for use where there was no platform, and of course, the Royal Arms, and those of the most distinguished orders of Chivalry, were hand-painted on the lower quarters. Inside, things were very grand indeed. The Queen's day saloon was upholstered and lined in blue and white watered silk. Both walls and ceilings were quilted. The double floor was filled with granulated cork to deaden noise. The lower lamp-shades covered sprung candles for reading. In the Diamond Jubilee Year, 1897, electric reading lamps were fitted, but the Queen never could be persuaded to use them. (Years before, she had made an awful fuss about gas, installed with the best of intentions, but not found amusing.) Altogether, the old London and North Western Company's Queen's Carriage is now an exquisite relic of Victorian furnishing.

In the Queen's bedroom – as we can look at it now – a sculptured bow-pot simulates her own favourite bouquet of flowers. The Queen often shared her bedroom with one of her daughters; twin beds, with brass bedsteads, are firmly screwed to the floor. When the Queen was ready to sleep, the oil-pot lamps, still lit, were covered by heavy baize caps. The Queen's dressers had a compartment of their own, padded in silk, in a shade of old gold, but there were no proper beds for them. They could lie down on the sofas, or else sit up all night. A conspicuous item, still *in situ*, is the large electric bell by which the Queen could summon them. A similar one was mounted in the compartment of

John Brown, for many years the Queen's Highland ghillie (posthumously succeeded by a somewhat unpopular Indian. Albert Edward, Prince of Wales, cordially detested them both.) Through the further door of this servant's compartment we find a cubby-hole containing (curious combination) both a pantry and a lavatory.

The Queen and her ladies also had lavatories, and the Queen's, as we can still see, was particularly sumptuous, lit by frosted glass and containing twin wash-hand basins and a monumental valve-type water-closet (a domestic blessing which, for the rich, dated back to the 1770s). This really was a great advance. Maybe you will think these things are being over-emphasized, but by degrees train lavatories descended from the royal trains, through saloons-for-hire and early sleepers, down to ordinary carriages for the general public; first-class, and ultimately second and third. Only with them could a train be considered really civilised, though much earlier, the Americans, with their greater distances of travel, had put a sort of iron funnel through the car floor, in an 'annexe' at one end. They also made arrangements for washing in an iron basin with a cork stopper.

We know quite a lot of what early- and mid-Victorian carriages looked like because contemporary artists took quite an interest in them and their inmates. Many of their pictures have survived. At Utrecht there is Constant Capp's painting of a Belgian first-class compartment, with *ingénue* pair. Augustus Egg's *Travelling Companions* shows a lovely pair of identical female twins in a first-class of the 'fifties, and from that same decade came Abraham Solomon's famous pair of paintings called *The Parting* and *The Return*. In one of these last the subject is a poor little boy being taken by his sorrowing mother and sister to join his first ship, probably at Liverpool, in a hard and advertisement-plastered second-class. In the companion painting a dashing young man (presumably the same one) in gold-braided blue cloth, with a sword, is seen making eyes at a lovely girl in a first-class carriage. When this picture first appeared the young man and girl are sitting together while an elderly man,

The day saloon of Queen Victoria's carriage, built by the London and North Western Railway in 1869, and now preserved for posterity in the Museum of British Transport, Clapham

Artists' licence – a peculiarly phoney impression of Queen Victoria and family in transit

The Parting *and*
The Return *by*
Abraham Soloman

perhaps the girl's father, has fallen asleep. There was such a howl of critical protest, however, about the potential depravity of the scene that Solomon provided another more decorous version with the elderly man wide awake and sitting between the two young people. Meanwhile the notoriety of the first painting led to the commissioning of the several later versions.

At Birmingham there is Charles Rossiter's *To Brighton and Back for Three-and-sixpence*. It shows an open-sided excursion carriage which might have been superannuated third- or even fourth-class (for the London, Brighton and South Coast Railway put on the latter for a while, as did several other thrifty undertakings). The picture shows the inevitable hard low-backed seats, with in this case, a mixture of working-class and poor-bourgeois in their poor best, out to enjoy themselves for one day by the sea.

Slowly, slowly, the lot of passengers in general improved. A Scottish company, the North British Railway, put on the first real British sleeping car for the public, apart from various 'bed-carriage' arrangements, in 1873, between London and Glasgow, and in that same year first-class passengers could book a berth between London and Scotland

To Brighton and Back for Three-and-sixpence *by Charles Rossiter*

whether by East- or West-Coast Routes. Second, and even third-class lavatories, even though they were still unmentionable in polite conversation, appeared on ordinary British trains before the 1880s were out.

Now America, though 'rough' in the mid-nineteenth century, was, as we have already seen, much more realistic. It was an American, George Mortimer Pullman, who made practical experiments in 1859 (held up by the Civil War) and in 1865 brought a very powerful influence to railway carriage design. His name, though often pirated, was to become a household word.

For some years before, another American, Ross Winans or, at any rate, one of his family, had pioneered the car with an open gangway, mounted on a pair of pivoted trucks ('Bogies' in original English). It had become the traditional *American*

car, sneered at by Charles Dickens, endured – at its worst – by Robert Louis Stevenson, but basically excellent.

Pullman's 1865 car was a really admirable sleeper, appropriately named *Pioneer*. It was the first real *Pullman car*. It was not of stage-coach ancestry. It had an open gangway down the middle, and it stemmed from the American passenger canal-boat of the Eastern States, adapted to rail-borne trucks, or bogies. By day, the original type of Pullman sleeper was an open car with fore-and-aft seating. The middle of the roof was raised in a handsome clerestory, with glazed shutters to give both light and ventilation, often very ornately decorated in etched or coloured glass, and against the supporting rails of this the folding upper berths were locked up by day. By night, the opposing seats were pulled out to meet, and the upper berths let down, both sorts having proper bedding provided and heavy curtains dropping over the lot to preserve the proprieties; though many funny stories have been told over mistaken berths.

Very soon after came the *parlor car* (old English and still-current American spelling) which was for superior daytime travel only, on massive, overstuffed, and variously adjustable arm-chairs in finest plush (*French plush*, according to old Pullman specifications). Woodwork – and the cars were built entirely of timber, with fine decorative veneers – was exuberantly ornate. Lighting was by great bronze kerosene lamps, and heating by a closed-circuit hot-water system (the Baker Heater, oil-fired).

Pullmans having arrived in the United States – and soon after, Canada – in the late eighteen sixties, and consequently having been sampled by James Allport, the Great Man of the Midland Railway in England, they came to Great Britain in 1874 with Pullman as seller and Allport as buyer. Allport even got Pullman-built coaches, second- and third-class, for the use of the commonalty, which apparently would have nothing of them. In their brief existence, they provided our first real corridor train, with all-modern-convenience for everybody, in the United Kingdom. (One of the third-class cars, minus its wheels, survived at the back of Bedford Station until 1966.)

But the first-class Pullman sleeper, certainly thanks to the opening of the Midland-Scottish route in 1876, flourished for a long time, and the parlor car, in limited service, for much longer still. It is quaint that the first Pullman car between London and Brighton, a run taking 65 minutes in the late 1870s, was in fact, a sleeper. Its name was *Mars*, and its sleeping berths were locked up for several years – one of the curiosities of the history of combined business and mechanical engineering. Another, Pullman, auspiciously named *Globe*, also on the Brighton line, was the world's first railway vehicle to be electrically lit, in 1881. It perhaps represents a treble first – American car, English railway and French (Fauré) system of lighting by immense batteries below!

George Pullman's Pioneer *coach of 1865. The interior by day, and . . .*

. . . converted for sleeping at night

This Brighton line was one whereon, in England, the Pullman parlor car stuck more than anywhere else, lasting until 1972. In 1908 it was an entirely British-built and British-owned Pullman train, the *Southern Belle*, which in its day was presented as the 'Most Luxurious Train in the World'. In 1933 came an electric version, soon named *Brighton Belle*. Certainly both were extremely good, and in sixty minutes there was no time to get wearied of them as one might weary of even the best American Pullman on the long hike from Omaha to San Francisco!

Luckily we can learn a great deal about the interiors of the *Southern Belle* from a most gorgeous official booklet, illustrated in splendid colour by Fortunino Matania, and published by the Pullman Car Company to celebrate this inauguration of 1908. The new British Pullmans had stately, moveable arm-chairs. They were of various sorts; ladies' cars to which male escorts were admitted so long as they did not smoke; buffet-cars with real bars, and – blessed amenity – you could have a good meal brought to you wherever you sat in the train. Which brings us to the subject of eating.

A Pullman sleeper was given a kitchen as far back as 1867, in Canada. A kitchen-parlor car appeared in the States next year, and that was still a year before the building of Queen Victoria's train, thus unprovided, on the London and North Western Railway. In 1874 we provided pre-cooked meals in Pullman cars of the Midland Railway. In 1879 (Great Northern Railway) we had a Pullman parlor-smoker-diner with a proper kitchen on board. By 1891, dining facilities went even to the old, despised third-class on the Great Eastern Railway's York-Harwich Continental Express. (Before that in 1889, the third-class passengers had got those badly needed lavatories on the Scotch Expresses between London, Edinburgh and Glasgow.) The companies had reached the stage where they were providing something like a land-ship in which one could travel, eat, drink and sleep, whereas the first American transcontinental trains of 1869 stopped for meals on their long, long trundles. Electric light succeeded oil gas, which had superseded rape-oil, kerosene and coal-gas lamps, though as we saw with the pot-lamps, the older forms died hard.

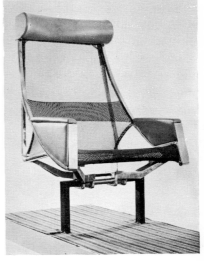

The chair designed for the British Advanced Passenger Train, compared with Pullman chairs of 1876

Revolution Year in Great Britain, was 1874, the year the Midland Railway first put stuffed seats in the third-class carriages and tried out the Pullman type. Rival companies were scandalized, but were very soon forced to keep up with the Midland. Apart from experiments, the fully-corridored train arrived in Great Britain on the Great Western Railway, in 1891; the same year as that of the Great Eastern's three-class dining set. Europe was to favour chiefly the side-corridors design with compartments, used in America only for superior sleeping cars.

Many odd sorts of sleeping car were tried before the European form finally set on that of compartments with side-corridor access to lavatories and, soon, to the rest of the train. That was through Georges Nagelmackers, a Belgian, who, with finance whipped up by Col. W. D. Mann (a wandering American) really established the Wagon-Lits fleet, starting this form in 1873. Single-berth cabins appeared on the East Coast Anglo-Scottish service in 1894, for all first-class comers. The third-class sleeper came to Sweden in 1910 (three berths in a tier) but long before that, the immense distances of Russia and America compelled provision of sleepers, of a Spartan sort, for the less-moneyed. Robert Louis Stevenson wrote gratefully about them on a Central Pacific immigrants' train in the late 'seventies, having previously endured for several days, the disgusting makeshifts of the Union Pacific company. Third-class sleepers with four-berth compartments came to Great Britain in 1928. Sometimes (couples were paired) the sexes got otherwise assorted, with comic results. The present British arrangement of single-berth first-class and double-berth second-class is fair enough, and much cheaper than some other people's.

Good heating, good ventilation and good beds are the three essentials. Heating by stoves, as in America, Russia and Scandinavia, is ancient. We have already noticed the old Baker hot-water heater. Low-pressure steam heating from the locomotive arrived in Great Britain about the turn of the century. Fearsome *footwarmers* (flat iron cans filled with boiling water and later ones with stewed soda-acetate) had long preceded it. They stuck to your boots and gave you heat-ache. Basic ventilation was by the windows, later supplemented by 'air extractors' in the roof, which we still use, or by hit-and-miss things in door-tops and clerestories. But right back in the 1870s air-cooling arrangements, using air-scoops with overhead cisterns and tumbler-fed water-curtains, were being built for the British-owned Indian trains. In North America, whose climate varied from that of Upper Canada in winter to that of Arizona in summer, long years saw plucky experiments in air-conditioning, as it is now called, but it did not properly arrive until the 1930s. Electro-mechanical means ultimately did the job.

As to beds; there are good beds and bad ones, a truth that applies whether in house, vessel, or vehicle. If railway undertakings wish to keep overnight passengers who otherwise may fly by day, they can do it by providing good beds because then the whole day can be saved. For the air passengers history seems to be moving in reverse – thanks to the prodigious speeds of air travel the flying-sleeper has already vanished into the past and people now sit up – or back – at night, as did the railway passengers for so many years.

Now the future of the passenger train seems to lie in two categories. There are the commuter trains in and out of great cities (nobody particularly loves them, though London's are nicer than those of Paris, Tokyo, New York and some others') and there are the fast inter-city trains in a densely-populated country, taking a couple of hours or so by day, or all night over longer stretches. For the latter the advanced passenger seat is all-important on the day services, and even overnight it is tolerable, as people tolerate it on long-distance aircraft. Again, its origins are ancient, probably derived from the adjustable seat in a chair-car (classless America's equivalent to the European first-class coach) and further back still from that often-feared though basically comfortable thing, the *dentist's* chair. Those designed for the British *Advanced Passenger Train* are of this order. The prototypes are not elegant, as eighteenth-century

French and English chairs, or the best of the early Victorians', were elegant, but they are practical. You can adjust them to your preferred attitude by pushing knobs and things, even while you are sitting in them.

Acknowledging such good things as the *Mistral* in France, possibly the real precursor of the inter-city train of the future is in the designs built for the new Tokaido line in Japan. The design is most scientifically carried out, with a minimum of weight and ornament, plus ease of access and egress. It seems that in vehicular furnishing there is to be little difference between the seating of aircraft or surface vehicle, of whatever sort, even if older people think back fondly to the ordinary European first-class carriage, internally sprung and stuffed, or to a plushy American parlor- or chair-car.

In discussing carriage design people often forget the design of the suspension – which includes springing – unless they are being cruelly bumped about in some worn-out old vehicle. From pre-railway days we have used the laminated or canti-lever spring. The railway simply took it over, using also spiral and volute springs for bogies and axles. Pendulum suspension of vehicles, adjusting itself to both gravitational and centrifugal force, as on curves, was being experimented with in the 1930s. It entails a good deal of mechanical complication. We all know how a vehicle, going rapidly round a curve, tends to fly off at a tangent. To counteract this, roads are *banked* and railways have their outer rails *superelevated*. But while the wheels stay put, the body still tends to tilt outwards, and the pas-senger's body is thrown even more abruptly towards the perimeter. Pendulum suspension gives the vehicle's body more to gravity and less to centrifugal force, with a consequent improvement in the comfort in travel and a great lessening of fatigue. When an aeroplane moves around a curve it solves this problem very easily by banking – for an earthbound vehicle quite elaborate mechanical means must serve the same end. And now, at last, the experiments seem to be flowering into practical applications on the new generation of railway carriages.

All these changes in carriage design, however fascinating they may be to the technical historian, are not simply stages in the 'evolution' of engineer-ing. They signal also progressive changes in social attitudes that have come a long way from 'Stan-hopes' to the point where the comfort of the 'ordi-nary traveller' is a primary concern of any competi-tive railway.

Interior of a coach on the Japanese Tokaido line

Railway architecture: small stations

DAVID LLOYD

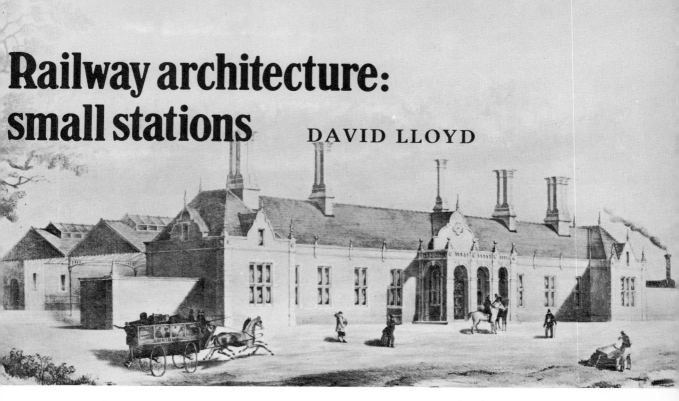

Arriving by horse-drawn coach at Louth Station

The coming of the railway gave rise to a new type of building – the railway station – for which there was no historical precedent. The earlier form of passenger transport, stage-coaches, made their starts and stops at coaching inns, which were related to the public road system. Railway trains ran on entirely new, separate and privately promoted systems, for which every item of equipment, and every associated structure, had to be specially provided. Stations were the points of contact between the public world of the streets and highways, and the private realm of the railways.

Until the invention of the motor-car, electric tram and motor-bus, railway stations had to be reached by horse-drawn transport, or else on foot. So they were usually built at relatively short intervals – every two or three miles, or less where the population was relatively dense. They varied enormously in scale from the great metropolitan termini like St Pancras, and huge junctions like Crewe, to tiny wayside stations serving single hamlets or a few scattered houses. This chapter deals mainly with the smaller stations (the larger ones form the subject of the next chapter), but discusses also the problems of conserving the more remarkable examples of station architecture, large and small.

The Stockton and Darlington Railway of 1825, on which the passenger trains were at first mainly horse-drawn, had only tiny cottages alongside the lines, where bookings were made; one such cottage survives at the site of the original terminus in Stockton-on-Tees. The Liverpool and Manchester Railway of 1830, the first regular passenger steam-operated line, provided the first buildings which we today can recognize as stations. One survives, at least in part, in Liverpool Road, Manchester – the prototype of all city terminals.

A very early example of a small country station survives at Wylam on the line from Newcastle to Hexham in Northumberland, which was opened in 1835. (Wylam happens, by an appropriate co-incidence, to have been the birthplace of George Stephenson.) The station of 1835 was a house, built in local stone in an imitative Tudor style (for this was the age of the early Gothic Revival), facing directly on to the line. Here lived the local head railwayman, or station master, and his family. At one corner of the house is a hatch, where intending passengers paid their money. That, at first was all; the passengers climbed direct from ground level on to the trains; no shelter was provided for them. But, by the early 1840s, railway companies came to have greater regard for the comfort of their passengers, even at small country stations. Platforms, of an appropriate height for boarding and leaving trains, came to be invariably provided; at Wylam one was constructed by about 1845, and behind it a small waiting room.

From the 1840s to the 1930s thousands of small or medium-sized stations were built which conformed to the same general pattern, though varying infinitely in detailed treatment. They contain one or more platforms, depending upon the number of tracks — often a station built originally to serve a single track would be later enlarged when the line was doubled or even quadrupled. Facing the principal platform (or the only one if the track is single) is a building usually containing a booking hall and a booking office (intercommunicating through a hatch), a general waiting room (and sometimes an extra one for ladies), a parcels office, perhaps a separate staff room, and toilet facilities for passengers and staff. Very often, though not invariably, these facilities are structurally integrated with the station master's house, though sometimes this is a separate building. The platform itself is sheltered by a canopy, usually extending over the whole width of the platform from the station building to the edge of the track. This is supported either by pillars and cross beams of wood or metal or, in many of the smaller examples, on brackets of wood or metal affixed to the wall of the station building. Where there is more than one platform there is generally a passenger footbridge (occasionally a subway), and some of the facilities provided in the main station building, particularly waiting rooms, are repeated on the other platforms. There were goods yards near to most stations, and

these often had their own goods or engine sheds, built separate from, but frequently grouping with, the main station buildings. Invariably there are, or were, signal boxes, located in the most convenient positions in relation to train operation.

This pattern of facilities on smaller stations was almost standard for a hundred years, but the variations in constructural form, architectural style and details are infinite. In the early part of the railway age, railway companies often employed architects for their stations who also practised in designing houses, churches or other more traditional types of building. Local materials were used for early railway buildings — stone from local quarries, bricks from local kilns, timber in the districts where a tradition of timber building existed. The architects varied their styles for the station buildings as often as they did for private houses — Gothic, Jacobean, Classical, French or Flemish Renaissance — according to their or their clients' fancies. For the platform canopies there was less traditional precedent, and sometimes these have a simple functional elegance, with their substructure of pillars, beams and brackets, and their perforated barge-boards overhanging the lines, given fretted edges in order to facilitate the dripping of water and prevent the timber from rotting. But even under canopies stylistic references crept in — metal capitals were moulded as if they were Gothic and of stone; iron brackets had openwork patterns like medieval tracery. Later in the railway age, companies tended to employ full-time architects who had no outside practice, or entrusted their station designs to their engineers. On the whole (and this is a generality, with plenty of exceptions) later railway stations — with their more standardised designs according to the style of each company, and their non-local materials, transported from anywhere by the railways themselves — are less interesting than the earlier examples.

One of the most interesting of early railway architects was Francis Thompson, an enigmatic figure of whom very little was known until recently. The researches of Mr Oliver Carter and

Wylam Station, opened in 1835 and still surviving

Battle Station, built in 1853 with a strongly monastic flavour

Great Malvern 1859. The capitals, cast in iron, are reminiscent of the stonework of medieval cathedrals

Gosport Station built in 1842 to serve Portsmouth across the water – but now a ruin

others have revealed that he was a tailor in the fashionable West End of London, who took to architecture as a second profession and was employed by at least three companies – the North Midland in Derbyshire and Yorkshire; the Chester and Holyhead; and the company operating the line from London to Cambridge. His station designs vary enormously in style, from the beautiful simplicity of Wingfield in Derbyshire (1840, closed) with elementary Classical proportions but almost no detailed elaboration, to the florid and complex Jacobean style of his great station at Chester. At Holywell Junction in Flintshire (1848, closed) he designed a station like a simple Italian villa (not as inappropriate a model as might be thought at first sight, since the upper floors of the main building comprised, according to the common pattern, the station master's house), with refinements at platform level, such as, for instance, the treatment of the arch and window frames, which help to make it a design of supreme elegance. At Audley End in Essex (1843) the design is very similar but rather simpler, except that the entrance from outside is protected by a large carriage porch, with rounded arches, for the convenience of Lord Braybrooke, his family and guests at neighbouring Audley End House, which the station served.

The station at Roydon, in Essex, built in 1842–3, almost certainly to the design of Francis Thompson, survives as a little altered example of a very small country station from the first days of railways. It is built of wood: timber-framed and faced in part with boarding, in part with plaster, following very much the centuries-old tradition of vernacular cottage architecture in south-west Essex of which several examples can be seen in Roydon itself and neighbouring villages. The main station building is a simple rectangle of a single storey, but it is given grandeur externally by an elegant porch, arc-shaped, with a wooden canopy, perforate-edged, supported on thin octagonal pillars. The platform canopy is supported by what might appropriately be called a gallows-type sub-structure, with diagonal wooden struts. Despite the general simplicity, the details are refined; for instance the door

Roydon Station – the entrance porch

and window openings, which make a regular symmetrical pattern on both the external and platform façades, are edged with finely moulded timberwork. The simplicity of Roydon is deceptive; though it owes so much to the traditional pattern of vernacular building in the neighbourhood, it was the work, not of unknown local craftsmen but of a sophisticated architect. In these respects it is typical of a surprisingly large number of smaller early stations.

Roydon Station – the platform canopy

Other notable architects who worked for early railway companies are W. Livock, on the London and North-Western, and G. T. Andrews, who designed many of the stations on the York & North Midland system controlled by George Hudson, the so-called Railway King. Few of Livock's stations have survived later rebuilding, but there is one on the main line at Atherstone, in Warwickshire, of red brick and with many gables. The more florid station at Woburn Sands on the Bletchley to Bedford line (1846) may have been by him too. Andrews had a widespread architectural practice based on York – the very fine former headquarters building of the Yorkshire Insurance Company in St Helens Square, York, dating from about 1845, is by him. His stations are sometimes in a severe, simplified Classical style, as at Malton (1845) and Pocklington (1847, closed), and sometimes in picturesque Gothic, as at Richmond, Yorkshire (1847, closed), which was designed with reference to the magnificent medieval castle. All these three, incidentally, are remarkable among smaller stations in that the tracks are covered by overall roofs – a form of construction usually associated with the much larger city terminals and junctions.

Most of the great railway engineers were not themselves architects, but I. K. Brunel, in this as in so many other respects, was exceptional. He certainly designed the original, and still surviving, terminal building at Temple Meads, Bristol (1841) as well as the contemporary, but much altered, station at Bath (now called Bath Spa). It is very likely that he designed the great majority of the stations along the lines in the West Country for which he was the engineer, although absolute proof of his authorship is usually impossible to find. Stations far and wide along Brunel's lines have many resemblances, both in style and details. Many are in an austere, simplified Classical style, using local stone or timber – Frome in Somerset, entirely built of wood (and with an overall roof like Andrews' stations in Yorkshire) is a good example. Others are in variants of the Tudor or Jacobean style he employed at Bristol and Bath. An example of these is at Bradford-on-Avon in Wiltshire (probably built about 1847, although the line it is on was not actually used until a few years later). This station is constructed of the local Bath stone, and, with its steep gables and its Jacobean style mullioned windows, it has a strong affinity with the numerous seventeenth-century cottages in the town, built when it was a great centre of the weaving industry. The canopies at Bradford are distinctive, being supported on elegant elongated brackets of iron, and the canopy edges lack the perforation usual elsewhere, but (as in several other of Brunel's stations) have a clean, smooth edge, giving the overall design a strong horizontal line which adds to its distinction.

An even more elaborate, small-scale station is Battle, in Sussex, built in 1853 to the design of W. Tress. Battle is famous for the remains of its medieval abbey, built on the battleground of Hastings, so the architect, with typical mid-Victorian romanticism, decided to give the station a strongly monastic flavour. It is an irregular building, built in the local stone, with gables of various sizes and windows with ecclesiastical tracery. Within the booking hall are two Gothic arches. The only un-monastic feature is the platform canopy, but even here the fretted bargeboards and supporting iron work are treated with more than usual elaboration.

The ultimate in platform ironwork is provided by Great Malvern in Worcestershire (1859) where the main station building is in a rather simpler version of the Gothic style of Battle, but the ironwork under the canopies is without parallel in Britain. The capitals of the supporting pillars are cast in a wonderful variety of vegetable forms, with delicately flowing leaves and stems reminiscent, in the medium of iron, of the stonework of medieval cathedrals. The architect, E. W. Elmslie, did indeed design churches – St Thomas' at Winchester is a good example of his work. And (just as happened in many churches during medieval times) the capitals of Malvern were brilliantly coloured, principally in blue and red. In a recent redecoration of the station, which does British Rail credit, the colours have been restored to their original glory.

Not all early stations were Gothic or Jacobean; some architects remained faithful to the long Classical tradition in English architecture. Sir William Tite, architect of the Royal Exchange in London, designed the suave stucco façade of the original terminal station at Southampton (1839, closed), which has a strong affinity with the slightly earlier Regency terraces nearby. At Gosport, where the station (1842) is now in ruins, Tite designed a magnificent Doric colonnade in Portland stone, now looking almost like a Roman ruin against the rank background of the vegetation which is taking hold of the remains of the station. The splendour of Gosport is due to the fact that in its heyday it served Portsmouth across the water – Portsmouth with its admirals – and Queen Victoria, who may have used the station on her way to review the Fleet.

Gosport is a sad ruin awaiting (we must hope) a redevelopment scheme for the site which would at least incorporate the superb colonnade. Two other outstanding Classical stations, at Huddersfield (1847) and at Monkwearmouth, now part of Sunderland (1848) have been rescued by their respective municipalities and restored. The station at Huddersfield is still open, but the train services have been so reduced that retention of the magnificent Corinthian forebuilding, forming the centrepiece of the town's main square, was considered by British Rail to be uneconomic. The town council decided to buy it to commemorate the centenary of the borough's incorporation, and now it stands cleaned and more splendid than it has ever looked since the grime from the Victorian mill chimneys first polluted its stonework.

Monkwearmouth Station, closed a few years ago, was not large, but it was given a disproportionate façade, with a magnificent Ionic portico, to commemorate the election of George Hudson as Member of Parliament for Sunderland in 1845 only three or four years before his financial downfall and subsequent disgrace. Now bought by the town council after a long and protracted negotiation with British Rail, it is being restored as one of the town's chief architectural monuments.

Not all public authorities are as enlightened as the town councils of Huddersfield and Sunderland in their desire to preserve fine railway architecture. British Rail itself refused to contemplate the preservation of the unique Euston Arch (of which more is written in the next chapter), as part of the new station complex. The hard headed businessmen of London and Birmingham in the 1830s were prepared to spend money on a pure monument; the executives of British Railways in the 1960s were not prepared even to keep it.

Birmingham's equivalent of Euston – Curzon Street Station, designed by the same architect, Philip Hardwick, at the other end of the original line out of Euston – may yet be saved. The three-storeyed station building, fronted by a fine Ionic portico, has not been used by passengers since the original New Street Station was opened in 1854, but was used as a goods office till recently. Now redundant, British Rail sought to demolish it but, as it is listed as a building of special architectural and historical interest, they had to obtain planning permission, which Birmingham City Council refused. A public inquiry was arranged, but cancelled at the last moment, at British Rail's request. Now it stands empty, awaiting a decision on its future.

Not all old railway stations are worthy of preservation as historic monuments when they become redundant, not even most of them; perhaps under five per cent are so good as works of architecture that thought, effort and expenditure are justified in trying to find means of keeping them from being demolished. Most of the stations mentioned in this chapter and the next, which are a selection from Britain's outstanding examples of railway architecture, come into this top category, of the five per cent or less. Many of them are already closed and empty; few have been so fortunate as those of Monkwearmouth and Huddersfield in being taken over by sympathetic town councils for restoration. Some might be converted for commercial, or even residential use (remembering that substantial parts of station buildings were often the station masters' houses).

Even the stations still in operation are often in danger; British Rail understandably wants to keep its facilities up to date and, in order to achieve this, rebuilding or drastic alteration is often commercially justifiable. The existing station building at Roydon, for example, is due to be superseded by a new building on the opposite side of the tracks, but the local people are striving to find a new owner and a new use for the present elegant station. Newcastle Station, most magnificent and historically significant of all great city stations, is threatened – British Rail are contemplating tearing down the train shed though retaining the façade, a threat that ought already to have caused a public outcry.

The uncertain fate of many magnificent railway stations is poignantly illustrated by that at Maldon, in Essex. Built at the end of a branch line in 1846, it was closed a few years ago, but it is still intact – just. Like several other stations in East Anglia (Stowmarket in Suffolk is a good example) it looks from the outside like a small Jacobean country house, with its round arched loggia, its big mullioned windows framed in stone, contrasting with the red brick of the walls, and its fretted Flemish style gables. The platforms are grass grown, the slender enriched ironwork supporting the extensive canopies is rusting. It is protected by being 'listed', but that does not prevent decay, and so far no potential buyer has expressed interest in converting and conserving it. Probably its position makes this prospect difficult – it is in the middle of an industrial estate and the number of possible commercial occupants who could make good use of this building in this particular location without drastically altering it must be very limited. In acutest form, Maldon illustrates the dilemma confronting those who would like to conserve the less than five per cent of all station buildings which really are outstandingly good of their kind.

The approach to Maldon East Station

Railway architecture: great city stations

J. M. RICHARDS

The large mainline station differs from the country station in more than size; it has to serve so many other purposes besides catching trains that it presents complex planning problems which make it more like a small town than a single – or, as in the case of most small stations, a divided – building.

The large station must provide space for crowds to assemble and for different categories of people to circulate without getting in each other's way: passengers and people meeting them and seeing them off, porters and others handling mail, parcels and baggage, and the engineering, administrative and service staff. And it must cater for many activities besides those which all stations are concerned with, which are mainly selling tickets, giving passengers somewhere to wait in comfort, giving them information about when trains leave and where to, and handling baggage and parcels.

The large station is, in addition, a shopping centre for books, newspapers, cigarettes, chocolates and flowers; it is a catering centre, with bars and restaurants, and above all an administrative centre. It is one of the places from which the railway is run. It has offices where business of many kinds is conducted out of sight of the public; it has accommodation for many grades of staff and, if it is a terminus or serves a major city, it may have a hotel attached to it as well.

In any case, with all these activities going on under one roof – or a succession of roofs – it is likely to be a monumental piece of architecture, of a size that will give it a big impact on its locality. Indeed stations were deliberately designed as monumental architecture, both to add prestige to the railway building enterprise and to make them landmarks in the cities they served, to which the coming of the railways was to bring new trade and a new industrial significance. Nevertheless, the railway station rarely occupies so central a position as a city's other public buildings. When the railways were built, it was seldom practicable to bring them into the middle of established cities; they skirted the edge, and the station was sited where it was most convenient for access. By now, however, it is often no longer so evident that the station was built away from the city centre because its presence has attracted growth and a new commercial centre has grown up round it.

Although a large railway station is made up of so many and such complex elements, the train shed, which is the high roofed space enclosing the tracks and their separating platforms, where arriving and departing trains can stand under cover, can usually be seen as something quite different and distinct from the remaining buildings. The train shed has been the railway station's main contribution to the many new structural forms that emerged during the nineteenth century. Being large and lofty it unifies the whole complex if anything can.

As in the small station, the other buildings are more conventional, conforming to the architectural fashions of their day. For obvious reasons of convenience, they are usually disposed on either side of the train shed, though the principal public elements like booking offices will all, for equally obvious reasons, be on the same side as the approach to the station from the city. Only in the case of a terminal station is a different grouping practicable.

The first train sheds were literally what the term suggests: a shed for trains to stand in, purely functional and often fairly primitive. One of the

93

earliest, the train shed at the London and Birmingham Railway's terminus at Euston, built in 1836, had a series of simple sloping roofs of wooden boarding supported on iron trusses which spanned between rows of cast-iron columns. Such was the inventiveness and initiative, however, of the railway builders that it was not long before these simple structures were developed into something more ambitious.

They also became more consciously architectural, since the pride that was taken in the construction of the railways, and the important part they were evidently going to play in the growth of the nation's economy, led to their being treated with an increasing degree of architectural display. A unique – but still relatively early – example of this is the train shed that the great engineer I. K. Brunel, the creator of the Great Western Railway, built in 1840 for Temple Meads station, Bristol. It has a hammer-beam roof in timber, elaborately designed in the Tudor style even before this had become generally fashionable among architects. It had a span of 72 ft., 4 ft. more than Westminster Hall. It was a wonderfully romantic conception,

and there is nothing else like it. It is now disused and has been made into a car park.

The real break-through in the structural form of the railway station came ten years later, when Newcastle Central was built for the York, Newcastle and Berwick and the Newcastle and Carlisle railways. The architect was a local man, John Dobson, who was responsible for many of the city's best buildings. He produced an unprecedented design for the Newcastle train shed which was to influence many others, first in Britain and then all over the world, and to endow the railway station interior with that sense of drama for which many large stations soon became notable.

This train shed used for the first time arched iron ribs to create a high vaulted roof, filled with glass that allowed sunlight to stream down into all parts of the station, producing beautiful atmospheric effects. Later British stations with similar roofs include those at New Street, Birmingham (1854), with a clear, single span of 211 ft., Paddington (1854), Charing Cross (1862), Cannon Street (1866) and Liverpool Street (1874), all in London, Liverpool Central (1874), Manchester Central (1880) and

York Station. The curved, glass and iron vaults designed by Thomas Prosser

Huddersfield Station, built in 1847

eventually Barlow's vast roof at St Pancras, London (1876), spanning no less than 243 ft.

York is perhaps the most impressive of these, since the plan of the station is curved, which, with the glass and iron vaults, produces remarkable effects of perspective, with arch receding beyond arch. As in the others, the detail has a Gothic flavour with moulded or foliated capitals and open-work spandrels like tracery. This accorded with the fashion of the time; it was favoured by engineers as well as by style-conscious architects and helped to give these great arched roofs their cathedral-like atmosphere. York station was designed by Thomas Prosser. It's on the same main line as Newcastle but dates from more than twenty years later because it was built to replace an earlier terminal station inside the city walls.

Both Newcastle, the pioneer, and York, its most spectacular follower, remain much as they were a hundred years ago, although – at Newcastle especially – the wide sweep of platform space has become cluttered by the addition of numerous kiosks and other small structures. The long, low station buildings still however allow the roof to dominate over everything.

The outside of Newcastle Central station again illustrates the contrast between the new structural forms created for the train shed roofs and the conventional academic architecture of the other buildings; but it is a handsome neo-classical affair, indicating the acceptance, by the middle of the nineteenth century, of the idea of a railway station as a civic monument. It is nearer than usual to the city centre and makes an important contribution to Newcastle's architectural dignity.

It is not, however, wholly as Dobson designed it. He meant it to have a portico running the whole length of the entrance façade, but this had to be omitted, after construction of the station had already begun, to make room for more offices when the directors decided to transfer the headquarters of the railway company to Newcastle from York. The present smaller portico was added by Thomas Prosser in 1840.

In two other north of England examples of the monumental, neo-classical station exterior – Huddersfield (1847) and Monkwearmouth, near Sunderland (1848) – the entrance portico is more successfully integrated with the design of the building. Monkwearmouth is believed also to be by Dobson. It may seem surprising for so relatively small a town to have such an imposing station but, as mentioned earlier it was built to celebrate the election of George Hudson, the Railway King, as member of Parliament for Sunderland. Huddersfield station is by James Pritchett, and simply as a work of architecture is the most distinguished of them all – with the possible exception of the first Newmarket Station, now disused, which has a long Baroque façade like that of a seventeenth-century orangery.

One more of these scholarly academic exercises should be mentioned again here for its symbolic, as well as its architectural, quality. This is Curzon Street, Birmingham, designed by Philip Hardwick in 1836, whose elegant Ionic portico was built to mark the end of the line from Euston and was thus the counterpart of the great Doric portico at Euston itself, demolished in 1962. Today the Birmingham portico is threatened as well. The Curzon Street station was abandoned for passenger traffic when, only twenty years after it was finished, the main line was extended beyond Birmingham, and was later used only for goods. Though it has been somewhat spoilt by later additions, it is still one of the best things Birmingham possesses.

Returning to London, we find at King's Cross, the terminus of the Great Northern line that serves the splendid stations at Newcastle and York, almost the only exception to the usual rule whereby the engineering structure, and especially the train

shed, at a major station is given a more self-consciously architectural frontispiece of the kind exemplified at Newcastle, Huddersfield and Monkwearmouth. King's Cross is a remarkable example of a great station with its internal structure perfectly represented by its exterior. The train shed is a great double arch of iron and glass supported on elegant brick piers, and the simple brick façade to Euston Road, with its two arched apertures separated and flanked by massive brick buttresses, exactly reflects this.

Designed by Lewis Cubitt in 1857, it splendidly represents that functional tradition in architecture that emerged so powerfully in all kinds of buildings – warehouses, docks, textile mills – which arose out of the Industrial Revolution, and to which the railways contributed their own quota in the shape of bridges, viaducts, engine houses and station verandahs as well as in the shape of the station train sheds referred to here.

The weakest part, perhaps, of the King's Cross façade is the relationship of the clock turret to the great bulk of the remainder (the clock, incidentally, was taken from the Crystal Palace when it was removed from Hyde Park to Sydenham Hill), but it is still a masterpiece of its kind. It still stands as it was built, though it has suffered for many years

Kings Cross Station. The double arch of the train shed shows clearly in the design of the simple brick façade

Left: an early photograph of the interior showing one of the two great arches

The Ionic portico of Curzon Street, Birmingham

John Dobson's original designs for Newcastle Central Station. The first train shed with an iron and glass vaulted roof

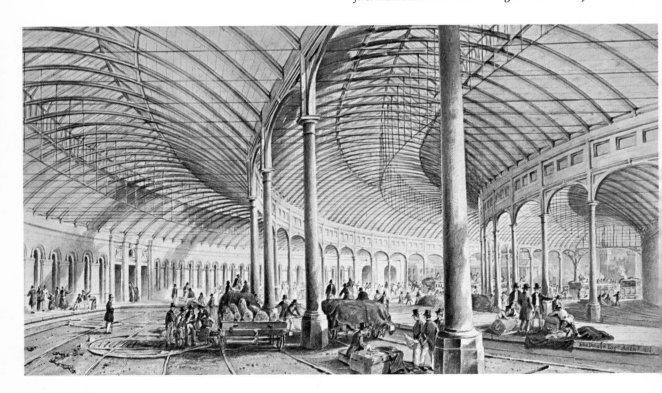

from a huddle of small buildings that clutter up the foreground. These are now being cleared away and replaced by a new glazed concourse one storey high which it is to be hoped will not obscure the view of the old station.

Alongside King's Cross stands another terminus that provides a remarkable contrast to it both in conception and style. St Pancras, built for the Midland Railway and completed in 1876, is the most spectacular example of a purely functional train shed – itself of monumental character on account of its vast size – hidden behind an ambitious architectural frontispiece, in this case the station hotel, but not unfortunately now used as such. The two elements are quite unrelated; indeed they were independently designed, the one by two engineers, W. H. Barlow and R. M. Ordish, the other by the most fashionable and successful architect of his day, Sir George Gilbert Scott.

Scott's hotel is an exuberant exercise in Gothic, using a confident amalgam of Italian, French and English models. It is built of dark red brick with dressings of Ancaster stone and grey and red granite. With the help of a profusion of towers and pinnacles and an intricacy of surface detail, it builds up, especially in the view from the west along Euston Road, into a composition that is unique in London.

It is not true, by the way, though the legend is often repeated, that Scott used for St Pancras a design he had first made for the Foreign Office. The truth is simply that he had wanted to do the Foreign Office in Gothic, and when Lord Palmerston insisted on a classical style Scott had already spent some time on the Continent studying Italian and French Gothic. He naturally wanted to make use of this research, and resume his interest in experimenting with the Gothic style for public building, when he came to design St Pancras.

The whole of the station – railway tracks and all – is raised high above the ground, to the same level as the bridge that carries the railway into St Pancras over the Regent's Canal. Beneath the station is a vast undercroft, with a very impressive interior that the public never sees, used as a brewery store

and a goods warehouse. The station has a forecourt at the upper level, reached by a ramp from Euston Road. From it a tall archway leads beneath the end of the hotel. This was designed to allow carriages to drive right in and set their passengers down under cover, at the entrance to the booking hall. Other archways lead straight beneath the hotel into the station itself.

Walking through one of these we get a sudden and dramatic view of the huge glass roof of the train shed, whose functional forthrightness and technological refinement create a surprising contrast to the elaborate architectural make-believe of the hotel and station buildings. It consists of one great arch, 100 ft. high and spanning 243 feet, free of visible ties and with its curve springing straight from platform level. The fact that its lattice ribs meet at the apex in a hardly discernible point is all it has in common with the Gothic buildings surrounding it. The culmination of the series of arched station roofs which Dobson pioneered at Newcastle Central, St Pancras is one of the greatest spans ever constructed and has since been exceeded among train sheds only by three in America: that at Jersey City (1888) for the Pennsylvania Railroad, of 252 ft. span, and those at the Reading and Broad Street Stations (both 1893) at Philadelphia, of 256 ft. and 300 ft. span respectively.

The magnificence of St Pancras – of the great roof as well as the Gothic hotel – was partly showmanship: an attempt to overpower the station's competitor nearby – King's Cross. But it was more than that. It would not have been so splendidly designed simply to make King's Cross look insignificant. All the great railway stations were conceived as monuments, and were given every kind of treatment their architects could devise to make them appear as such. They stood for their creators' pride in the achievement the building of the railways represented, but what each was celebrating was more than a railway; it was a new stage in man's conquest of nature and the railway builders' own confidence that the process of conquest would go on for ever.

They celebrated this with all the architectural

panoply at their command, and they did so most impressively of all at the third great London terminus that stands alongside King's Cross and St Pancras – Euston; or used to stand, because this grandest of all railway termini has now been totally rebuilt. These three stations are in fact, together with Paddington to the west (which today looks its best after being cleaned and beautifully re-painted internally) the only big stations in London of real architectural distinction, though the train shed at Liverpool Street has magnificent scale and is capable of highly romantic lighting effects – enhanced by, rather than in spite of, a century of smoke and grime – and Cannon Street had, until the last war, some of the same kind of utilitarian nobility as King's Cross, and Fenchurch Street still has a graceful and agreeable façade.

Euston, however, was of a different order. Its great hall, and its granite entrance portico, both designed by Philip Hardwick, were among the most notable architectural achievements of the nineteenth century, and there were other fine

St Pancras Station, built in 1876. Sir George Gilbert Scott's exuberant exercise in Gothic hides a vast train shed with a huge glass roof.

interiors such as the Shareholders' Room. The great hall, completed in 1849, was in a robust Roman style with a coffered ceiling 62 ft. above the floor and a double flight of stone stairs, surmounted by Ionic columns, leading up to the surrounding galleries at one end of its 168 ft. length.

The hall's Roman style was chiefly contributed by P. C. Hardwick, Philip's son, but on the entrance portico Philip Hardwick worked alone. It was the last work, in fact, executed by him without his son's assistance and was a model of monumental simplicity. It was completed in 1840. It was built of granite, in the form of a Greek Doric propylaeum (not strictly a portico, and certainly not an arch, though often referred to as the Euston arch), 72 ft. high and flanked by pairs of lodges. It was its uncompromising severity, combined with its heroic scale, that made it so fitting a design to serve the symbolic purpose of London's gateway to the north.

There may have been sound arguments why the British Railways Board had to destroy the great hall when they rebuilt Euston Station ten years ago, but there was no need to destroy the propylaeum as well. Its demolition was a wanton act of vandalism that took place in spite of widely supported protests. So great in fact was the public outcry that the question of its preservation or destruction was taken to Cabinet level, and the decision to demolish it was made personally by the then Prime Minister, Mr Harold Macmillan.

The climate of opinion, as regards historic buildings, has since changed and it was a tragedy that would not, I believe, occur today. It was not even accepted that the stones of the propylaeum should be numbered to allow it to be re-erected on another site. This was doubly a tragedy since the rebuilt station has an empty paved space in front of it – an ideal setting for the propylaeum, where its powerful solidity would have made an admirable foil to the transparency of the somewhat featureless façade of the modern station and where it could have continued to play the visual and symbolic roles it was designed for.

Euston Station, the great hall and the propylaeum, both now destroyed

Uphill and round the bend

J. T. van RIEMSDIJK

The Rigi Railway poses for its photograph

A mainline railway is very carefully engineered to avoid steep gradients and sharp curves, because this enables it to handle heavy traffic at high speed. This, at least, is the ideal aimed at. But there are routes which are unavoidably difficult, and there are many main lines which have had to be built without the benefit of vastly expensive tunnels, bridges, and major earthworks or rock blasting. Many of these are overseas, in the developing countries, and are single tracks, and of narrow gauge, yet they still handle enormous loads.

There are also railways which climb mountains, because, as the mountaineer has said, 'they are there'. Many of these have no purpose but to reach the summit. Switzerland is the setting of many of these lines, and tourists provide most of their traffic, though a service to some of the precipitous hill farms comes as a bonus. In Britain, the Snowdon railway is the sole example.

For specially difficult railways like these, special types of locomotive were developed, the origins of which go right back to the first few years of steam locomotive history. John Blenkinsop, about the

year 1811, had the idea of a type of locomotive which, instead of driving its track wheels, would drive a gear wheel meshing with a continuous rack along the railway, and William Chapman, a year or two later, worked with Hedley to give *Puffing Billy* and its two stable-mates some sort of flexible wheelbase with all wheels driven. A little later, George Stephenson produced a sort of articulated locomotive by driving the leading tender wheels of *Blücher* by a chain from the engine.

These beginnings were not followed up, because better rails and a better understanding of adhesion showed them to be unnecessary for the railways then in use, and if a very steep gradient occurred on a railway, it was kept short and worked by cable traction. The ideas were not revived until the second half of the nineteenth century, and then it was appropriately Swiss engineers who played the leading part.

The idea of a mountain rack railway with steam locomotives was first effectively worked out by Nicholas Riggenbach, engineer of the Swiss Central Railway, and patented in 1863. He proposed a single rack, with upward pointing teeth, lying midway between the rails. The teeth were to be made to a geometrically correct form to ensure that the gear meshing with them would not attempt to climb out of them. This mean that the whole construction was rather costly. Perhaps for this reason he could not get the backing he required to build a railway, and had to bide his time.

In the meantime, in the United States, where an unsuccessful attempt had been made at a rack-fitted section on a freight line some twenty years earlier, Sylvester Marsh constructed a rack railway up Mt. Washington, in the Presidential range in New Hampshire, which started operation in 1869. This was at first operated by a vertical boilered locomotive with a large wooden cab of typically American aspect, named *Old Peppersass*, which is preserved on the railway, and, though not now used, it was steamed on the occasion of the line's centenary. The rack was a simple one made like a ladder, with round rungs, and the gear wheel under the engine was deep enough to ensure that two of these were in mesh all the time. All the same, as a precaution against the gearwheel lifting out of this rather primitive type of rack, rollers were fitted which bore upon flanges at the sides of the rack in such a way as to provide security.

Riggenbach lost no time in visiting this railway, and found on his return to Switzerland that the news of it sufficed to ensure backing for his own venture, and the first European mountain rack railway was built to the summit of the Rigi from Vitznau, on Lake Lucerne. It was opened in 1871,

A model of the mechanism of the Riggenbach locomotive, 1870

The steam railcar for the Pilatus Railway

also with a vertical boilered locomotive which is now preserved on the railway. Today, electricity is the motive power, as on most Swiss railways, but steam locomotives are still used in the height of the season, when the railway's use of electricity has to be restricted. Nowadays, the steam locomotives are an added attraction.

The maximum gradient on the Vitznau-Rigi Railway is 1 in 5, and 1 in 4 is usually taken as the steepest for which the single ladder type rack is suitable – in spite of which the Mt. Washington Railway, of less sophisticated design, climbs some sections as steep as 1 in 2·6. When a railway was planned to ascend Mt. Pilatus, again from the shores of Lake Lucerne, gradients of very nearly 1 in 2 were envisaged, and a new system was designed for the purpose by the engineer of the line, Edouard Locher-Freuler.

The Locher rack, as it is usually called, is unique to the Pilatus Railway. It consists of a single bar laid midway between the rails, having teeth machined in both sides, vertically. The vehicle – for in this case locomotive and carriage are one – has driving pinions arranged in a pair, one on each side of the rack, so there is no possibility of their ever coming out of mesh. A further pair of pinions is provided in connection with the braking system. This railway was opened in 1888 and operated, of course, by steam. The railcars, as we might call

The Pilatus Railway track

them today, had engines and boilers at the lower end, and a series of passenger compartments ranged above. These were (and still are in the electric railcars now used) arranged to be upright on the gradient, so they are stepped one above the next, and the platforms are in the form of flights of steps.

The ascent of Pilatus is probably the most hair-raising railway journey in the world. The track clings in places to a narrow ledge with a vast fall beneath and a sheer face above, winding steeply upwards into the curious mixture of wind and mist which so often shrouds the summit of Pilatus, and gives it its Roman name, meaning that it has hair on its head. At the summit it can sometimes be a relief to get back into the train for an hour-long journey down to a totally different climate. The whole Lucerne area is notorious for its rainfall, but the conditions on the Rigi are usually kinder, and the view unforgettable. Pilatus towers on the opposite side of the lake, its summit shrouded in turbulent mist, and all around are mountains, most of which have railways, but the only such thing visible, apart from the Rigi's own two (there is another rack railway climbing up from Arth Goldau) is the upper part of the lift which ascends

within the Bürgenstock but bursts out into the open near the top, to present the astonishing sight of a vertical lattice liftshaft high above the lake.

The Swiss have become the world experts of everything to do with mountain engineering, just as the Dutch, long before, became the experts on reclaiming land from water, and for the same reason. So it was to be expected that the sole British example of a mountain rack railway should be equipped with Swiss built locomotives, and built on a Swiss system, that devised by Dr Roman Abt. This has two racks, side by side, with the teeth staggered. The engines have two double pinions, each engaging with both racks, and spaced some way apart along the length of the machine. The spacing is such that the meshing of the two pinions with the rack is out of phase, which means that for each tooth-length negotiated by the engine there are four pinion teeth going into mesh one after the other. This produces a perfectly smooth action. As in all rack railways, the engine pushes the train up the gradient, and is not coupled to it. Similarly it supports the train when descending, using a counter-pressure action in the locomotive's cylinders to regulate the speed, this being linked to a centrifugal governor. The coaches have in addition their own automatic braking system applied through their own pinions meshing with the rack.

A model of the mechanism of the Snowdon Railway locomotive, 1896, using the Abt system

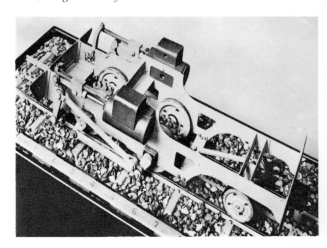

The Snowdon train today

The Snowdon Railway opened on Easter Monday, 6 April 1896. The second train met with disaster on the way down. Because of a severe frost followed by a thaw, part of the track had distorted, and the locomotive derailed, lifting its pinions clear of the rack. It plunged down a steep ravine and was totally wrecked. The locomotive crew jumped to safety, and the train, not being coupled to the engine was stopped quickly by the automatic brake. But unhappily a passenger took fright and jumped out to his death.

The Snowdon Railway derailment, 1896

When the railway was reopened, provision had been made, as on the Mt. Washington line, to ensure that the pinions could not lift from the rack. The rack is fitted with side rails (except at junctions, which are not on steep sections of the line) which engage with hook-shaped pieces beside the pinions, and the system is now as safe as that on Mt. Pilatus. The railway is immensely popular, and the route it traverses one of the most beautiful parts of the British isles. It is still steam worked, and although new locomotives have come from Switzerland since the opening, the original ones, with the one sad exception, are all still in use. The Abt system, moreover, is probably the rack system most in use in the world today.

One other 'extra grip' system must be mentioned, that due to the English engineer J. B. Fell. This is not a rack system at all, but employs a third, smooth rail in the middle of the running rails. Two smooth wheels arranged side by side under the locomotive and lying in a horizontal plane press against the two sides of this rail and provide adhesion to supplement that on the running wheels. After an experimental application in England in 1863, Fell proposed this system in a fully developed form for the old railway over the Mont Cenis Pass, which was entirely successful, though short lived because of the construction of the tunnel, for which this railway was merely intended as a short term substitute. The Fell system found application in many parts of the world, one of the best known places being the Rimutaka incline in New Zealand, where for many years quite small locomotives worked heavy trains up $2\frac{1}{2}$ miles of gradient as steep as 1 in 13. Quite recently, a new line has bypassed this stretch, at great cost, and normal locomotives can now work from Wellington right through to the north-east. The Fell system provided a useful intermediate between the normal adhesion railway and the rack railway and was appropriate for gradients between about 1 in 10 and 1 in 30. Great power is not usually required on very steep gradients, because they are climbed slowly. Quite light locomotives can therefore suffice, provided that they can get a grip on the track. A heavy locomotive wastes its extra power in lifting itself. The Fell system is suitable for higher speeds than a rack system, and does not involve special carriages. This makes it especially convenient for short sections of through routes.

There are many lines of railway worked by normal adhesion locomotives which yet present severe problems of gradient and curvature. How severe these problems are depends, of course, on the loads and speeds involved, and a curve which seems severe for a 15,000 ton North American freight train might pass unnoticed in a 400 ton British express. All the same, the problems and the solutions are much the same, regardless of scale, and a fascinating chapter in locomotive history tells the story of the special purpose machines built for difficult, often narrow gauge lines, and especially interesting is the development of articulated locomotives, among them the largest and most powerful units that ever ran on rails.

A first approach to the problem of running railways through mountain ranges and other terrain involving large civil engineering works is to adopt a narrow gauge. The railways of Africa are almost all of 3′ 6″ or 1 metre gauge, and if speed is a little lower than in Europe, loads are no less heavy. The whole railway system of Japan was also on the 3′ 6″ gauge until the new Tokaido line was built, and there are large mileages of narrow gauge in most continents of the world. The advantage of a narrow gauge is that it allows of sharper curves, for reasons concerned with the behaviour of wheels mounted in pairs rigidly on their axles, as is normal railway practice, and with the design of pointwork at junctions. This means that the railway can follow the contour lines of the landscape more closely, avoiding costly earthworks or rock-blasting, and also easing the gradients. The overall cross section of the train need be no smaller than that of a standard gauge train for these advantages to show themselves, but if it is smaller, then, of course, other advantages accrue, such as smaller tunnels and narrower ledges on mountain sides.

In the British Isles, perhaps the most attractive narrow gauge railway is that which runs up the Vale of Rheidol from Aberystwyth to Devil's Bridge, though Wales has other narrow gauge lines which might reasonably be considered its equal. The Vale of Rheidol is the last stronghold of the steam locomotive on the national system, and is worked by small, fairly orthodox, tank locomotives, which are really 60 cm. gauge versions of a standard gauge engine, pleasingly scaled down and with the slight and kittenish disproportion that follows from the fact that the driver and fireman have to be accommodated in a full-sized cab. The only noticeable constructional difference is that the main frames are outside the wheels, because these are close together, and the drive from the outside cylinders is onto small cranks on the axle ends. This type of engine was first ordered for the Vale of Rheidol line at the turn of the century, but was perpetuated in new engines built at Swindon by the Great Western, which absorbed the owning Cambrian Railways at the grouping of the railways in 1923. These engines weigh around 25 tons.

This railway is now purely a tourist line, but it was built to serve lead mines, and originally had the character of an industrial railway. The 60 cm. gauge is one especially associated with portable tracks such as are frequently used in quarries, and its use is world wide. The track of the Rheidol line is now laid to very high standards and gives a very smooth ride at quite high speeds, but a ride on it still gives a very good idea of the advantages of the narrow gauge. For much of the way, the railway clings to a ledge on one side of the valley, twisting and turning round the spurs and hollows of the steep valley wall. It climbs nearly 700 ft. in eleven miles, which is quite a severe gradient for a normal adhesion locomotive pulling a long train of bogie carriages, but nothing exceptional. The narrow gauge, in fact, makes possible a normal railway on a small scale, in a situation where a full-size line would be too expensive to be worth building. There are such lines in many parts of Europe, and most of them are, like the Rheidol line, in beautiful mountain settings.

On the Festiniog Railway, further north along

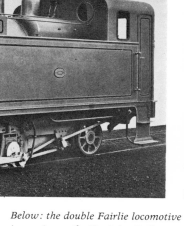

*Above: the Fell locomotive built in 1886
for the Rimutaka Incline, New Zealand*

*Below: the double Fairlie locomotive
in service on the Festiniog Railway*

*Above: the Vale of Rheidol train takes
water at Aberffrwd*

the Welsh coast, what must be the oldest articulated steam locomotives in service illustrate the problem of building a really powerful engine to go round sharp curves. The Festiniog is another 60 cm. gauge line, originally built to serve the slate quarries of Blaenau Ffestiniog in the 1830s. Not only is it, too, very beautifully sited, but it also is of outstanding historical interest from the technical point of view. One of its locomotives is now well over a century old, but still doing good work; it still operates its historic articulated locomotives; and the first bogie passenger coach ever to run in these islands is still available, a century later, to carry the sightseers who provide most of the revenue for this privately preserved railway.

The articulated locomotives are to the double-bogie, double-ended design of Robert Fairlie, an enthusiastic protagonist of the narrow gauge, as was James Spooner, who had laid out the line and managed it for many years. The origin of the Fairlie locomotive – at least in its double ended form – was clearly in the locomotive built by Cockerill, of Seraing, in Belgium, for the celebrated trials held by the Austrian government, in which a prize was offered in hopes of finding a type of locomotive suitable for working the Semmering inclines. Those trials were the genesis of several types of articulated locomotive, but none of the competitors on that occasion was wholly successful. When loads were small on lines with steep gradients and sharp curves, small locomotives were adequate, like the thousands of little four-wheeled quarry locomotives and industrial shunters still to be found all over the globe. When loads increased they could be worked in pairs, but little engines working hard ride roughly, and two of them coupled together ride even worse. Moreover, they required two crews. For the Giovi incline in Italy, Robert Stephenson, in 1855, built a special type of four-wheeled tank engine, intended to be used in pairs back to back, and coupled together with a special coupling designed to prevent oscillation between the two. A single crew could man both engines, as they had a common footplate, or one driver

A model of the large Fairlie built for Mexico by Neilson and Company in 1889

could drive them while two firemen stoked. These engines weighed only 13 tons each, but were considered very heavy in their time, and were nicknamed 'The Mastodons of the Giovi'.

After this, back-to-back locomotives were used in several countries, and the Fairlie locomotive was almost certainly prompted by their success, which made the designer have another look at Cockerill's Semmering engine of 1852. There had been something very similar in America twenty years earlier but it is unlikely that the news of that had come to the ears of either Cockerill or Fairlie.

The Fairlie locomotive, although there were a few single-ended machines which came later, consisted of a double-ended boiler, with two fireboxes in the middle and a smokebox and chimney at each end, all in one piece. The middle was surrounded by the cab, in which the driver and fireman stood on each side of the boiler, and could not, of course, cross to the other side. Water tanks and coal bunkers were attached to this assembly, which was carried on two swivelling trucks or bogies, each equipped with two outside cylinders. Some Fairlies had six-wheeled trucks, but the Festiniog engines, built in 1872, had four wheels at each end. This design was not without its faults, one of which was the need to convey steam to each swivelling engine unit by means of some sort of flexible connection, which had to be able to withstand the full boiler pressure. But the Fairlie engines generally rode very well, rather like carriages, and on the Festiniog, after long and chequered careers, two of them are still capable of very useful work, whenever heavy trains are needed, and longevity is normally an indication of quality in steam locomotives.

The Fairlies of the Festiniog actually weigh less than the more orthodox and shorter engines of the Vale of Rheidol, but all their weight is carried on driven wheels, so their ultimate haulage capacity is greater. Also, their weight is less concentrated, and this is important from the point of view of the strength of the track support, be it earthwork or a bridge. All recent electric and diesel-electric locomotives, apart from small shunters, have copied the layout of the Fairlie locomotive, some of them

even to the point of having the buffers and couplings mounted on the swivelling trucks, even though they may be intended for well-aligned main lines where the problems of the Festiniog are undreamed of. For the knowledgeable tourist, the double-ended engines give the Festiniog a special interest, for it is unlikely that any Fairlies survive in use elsewhere, and the sight of one of these pleasing machines winding its way up the beautiful slopes flanking the Glaslyn estuary, with steam puffing from both ends, is as memorable as it is historic.

Probably the most numerous of all types of articulated locomotive is the type invented by Anatole Mallet, a Swiss by birth but French by education, whose career was always closely associated with compound locomotives. He had, in 1876, built the first successful compound locomotives in history, some small tank engines for the Bayonne-Biarritz Railway in south west France. He conceived his articulated locomotives for exactly the sort of service for which Robert Fairlie conceived his, but the result was very different. The Mallet design has to be seen in terms of compounding, even though in later days it came to be built as a simple expansion engine because, in the high powers which the type had attained, it was not possible to fit low pressure cylinders of sufficient volume.

The Mallet type had (and still has, for numerous examples of the compound Mallet still exist) a complete high pressure engine, with two cylinders driving a set of coupled wheels, arranged under the rear end of the boiler. This was rigidly attached to the boiler and main framing, and the high pressure steam pipes did not have to be flexible, as on the Fairlie. Under the front end of the boiler a second engine was provided, with two low pressure cylinders driving a second set of coupled wheels. This was arranged with sideways movement, and was hinged to the rear engine, while the weight of the front end of the boiler was applied to it by a sliding bearing. Low pressure steam, exhausted after use by the high pressure cylinders, was fed to the low pressure engine via a large pipe provided with universal joints, which were not subjected to the boiler pressure as in the Fairlie type.

The advantage of this is clear enough. One flexible pipe connection is to be preferred to two, especially if the pressure in it is never more than about a third of full boiler pressure. Moreover, the Mallet type also required only one flexible exhaust pipe instead of two. The disadvantage of the type lay in the fact that the boiler always pointed in the direction in which the rear engine was travelling, and on sharp curves it went well off the centre of the track. It also possessed considerable inertia, and its obstinately tangential attitude could cause rough riding on curves unless the engine ran slowly. Eventually suitable springing and oscillation damping arrangements were arrived at, especially in the United States, where Mallet type engines sometimes ran very fast. But in spite of these difficulties the Mallet type was an admirable concept, well matched to the technological resources of its time, and capable of enlargement into the most enormous and powerful of all steam locomotives – far more powerful than any single unit diesel, and only matched by some articulated electrics.

The first Mallet articulated locomotives were for the 60 cm. gauge. This gauge of just under 2 English ft. had early become an international standard, but was particularly developed by the French firm of Decauville, which, originally a distilling concern, had in 1875 installed a 60 cm. gauge service railway, and thereafter became a great protagonist of the gauge, and the leading maker of equipment for it. In 1887 Paul Decauville ordered the first locomotives of the type, which had been proposed by Mallet two years earlier, and Mallet designed a 12 ton locomotive on four axles, ideal for the sort of industrial and secondary rural service in which the firm was beginning to specialise. Six were built, and first used in an exhibition in 1889, where they did very well, afterwards going to various small railways for further service. After this the type multiplied and became common on European secondary railways and in European

The first type of Mallet compound articulated locomotive, built in 1889 for the 60 cm gauge

colonies, in both of which types of service it is still to be found. It was not much used on main lines in Europe, where articulated locomotives were not really needed, and never used at all in England, but was frequently to be found climbing up tortuous tracks in mountainous country.

It was not until the first years of the twentieth century that the Mallet type began to be built in the United States, but from 1904 onwards it became more and more the typical American high powered locomotive, and its character changed in several ways. From being essentially a slow speed machine used for hard pulling (or pushing) on winding tracks, it blossomed into an express freight locomotive, and even a fast passenger one. So heavy are American trains that an orthodox, rigid framed, locomotive cannot always handle them – the sheer length and weight, necessary for the power, demands an articulated locomotive if it is to be able to negotiate the unavoidable sharp curves at junctions and in station yards. So the Mallet type was built at least as late as 1952, the last examples being, unusually for the period, compounds, and weighing 266 tons without their tenders. These engines worked 7,000 ton coal trains over easy stretches of main line at 50 m.p.h.

Halfway through the American Mallet story, in 1924, the simple expansion Mallet, with four high pressure cylinders, had appeared. There was by this time no difficulty in making the flexible steam connections, and the size of low pressure cylinder had reached its practical maximum early that year in some double ten-coupled engines built for the Virginian Railroad, with low pressure cylinders of 4 ft. internal diameter. The Pennsylvania Railroad some months later, produced an even more powerful engine, but this time with smaller cylinders on the front end, taking the full boiler pressure. At that time also, the design of valves and valve gearing, and of steam passages generally, was not as advanced as it later became under the guidance of the great French engineer, André Chapelon, whose compound locomotives surpassed all others in fuel economy and power-to-weight ratio. So it was found that the simple Mallet ran more freely at speed than the compound, and this factor undoubtedly led many companies to adopt this variation on Mallet's original concept.

So it was that the largest and most powerful of all steam locomotives was a four cylinder simple Mallet – the Union Pacific *Big Boy*. Twenty of these were built in 1941–4, and they developed some 10,000 horsepower in their cylinders. They had two sets of eight coupled driving wheels, with bogies at the front and under the firebox, which was the size of a room, nearly 20 ft. long. The tender was carried on 14 wheels, and the total length of engine and tender was of the order of 135 ft. Top speed was 80 m.p.h., but they also in regular service hauled trains of over 4,000 tons up gradients of 1 in 100, at about 20 m.p.h. So high was the temperature of the superheated steam that the pistons were found to glow red hot under some conditions of service. Though these engines are no longer in service, and their place has been taken by diesels, often five or six coupled together, yet so great has been their hold on the American

The Union Pacific Big Boy *4-8-8-4 locomotive in service*

imagination that most of them are still in existence, in private collections, or exhibited as National Monuments in public parks. No better tribute to American engineering could be found than these great engines, and none more fitting, in a country which was so largely created by the railroad.

The last articulated type to be described here was a British invention, and though not as numerous as the Mallet, of which over 3,000 were built in the U.S.A. alone, or built in any such enormous example as the 'Big Boy', locomotives of this type were perhaps the finest of all articulated engines, and certainly the fastest. Moreover, they are still numerous in the world, and doing some of the hardest work done on rails anywhere. This type was invented by Herbert Garratt, and became the speciality of the Manchester firm of Beyer, Peacock and Co. Ltd, a locomotive builder with a particularly distinguished record in the history of British railways, and one with a large overseas market.

In the Garratt locomotive, or the Beyer Garratt as it later became, there are two engine units, each free to swivel in accommodating itself to the track, and carrying buffers and couplings at its outer end. Slung between them, supported on pivots near the inner ends of the engine units, is a boiler on a cradle, which has no wheels beneath it, so it can be as large in diameter as the 'moving load gauge' of the railway allows. It can also have a large firebox, with a capacious ashpan. The freedom this gives to the boiler designer ensures a boiler which is ideally proportioned and not expensive to build, and this is really the supreme virtue of the Garratt type. But it also has the property of riding extremely well at the highest speed, a property best demonstrated in 30 engines built for express service on the Algerian State Railways, in the 1930s, which were required to sustain 75 m.p.h. over long distances. The total weight of these was more than 200 tons, their length over 100 ft., and they were built in France under licence and with the collaboration of Beyer Peacock.

The first locomotives of the type were two little eight wheelers for the 2 ft. gauge, built for Tasmania in 1908. Thus the beginnings were strangely like those of the Fairlie and the Mallet types. They weighed a little over 33 tons, and one of these was bought back by Beyer, Peacock sometime after it had finished its service because the railway had been closed down. This engine is now, following the closure of Beyer, Peacock's locomotive business, preserved on the Festiniog Railway, where it is hoped to adapt it to run on the tracks which have seen the pioneer articulated locomotive type, the Fairlie, for a century. The very first Fairlie and Mallet locomotives have not survived, so the preservation of this small Garratt is especially fortunate.

Perhaps the greatest event in the history of the Garratt type was the decisive comparison made with the Mallet on the South African Railways in 1921. A number of prototype Garratts were made,

one of which was for the heaviest duties on the larger, main line, gauge of South Africa, which is 3' 6". This locomotive weighed 134 tons and was compared with a large Mallet type weighing, with its tender, 180 tons. The Garratt locomotive, like all of its type, had no separate tender, water and fuel being carried over the engine units. In a full series of trials, the Garratt hauled slightly heavier trains, of around 1,000 tons, at a higher average speed and with a substantially lower fuel and water consumption, on a heavily graded and severely curving route. It was a decisive victory for the Garratt, and large orders for Garratt locomotives of various types followed. In fact, the most recent were delivered to the South African Railways in 1968. The performance of the prototype, class G.A., in these trials was undoubtedly studied in locomotive circles all over the world, and the subsequent success story of the Garratt type marked a welcome return of Britain to a leading role in international railway engineering.

The most powerful single locomotive on British railways was a Garratt built for the London and North Eastern Railway in 1925, which spent forty years banking trains up two famous gradients: the Worsboro incline in Yorkshire, used by heavy goods trains, and the Lickey bank outside Birmingham, where all sorts of trains have to ascend a long climb at 1 in 37. Its total weight was 178 tons, it had six cylinders, and a grate area of $56\frac{1}{2}$ sq. ft. It was if anything too powerful, and could never show its full potential on such intermittent work. The London, Midland and Scottish Railway had 33 Garratts of a somewhat smaller type, which were for long used on main line coal trains. These Garratts were the only articulated locomotives to see regular service on British main lines.

As a fitting conclusion to the story of the articulated locomotive, the largest locomotives in Australia are worth describing. 42 of these, plus another 8 delivered unassembled for use as spares if necessary, arrived from Beyer Peacock in 1952, and they are mostly still in service. Each engine unit has eight coupled wheels, with a four wheeled bogie at each end. They work on the standard 4' $8\frac{1}{2}$" gauge of the New South Wales Government system, and their extremely flexible wheelbase and multiplicity of wheels, to carry their great weight of 260 tons, makes them suitable for working routes where diesels of suitable power are still unacceptable, and would in any case have to be used in multiple. They are very handsome machines, equipped with mechanical stokers, essential with over 63 sq. ft. of grate, and many other modern aids to easy operation and maintenance. They move with extraordinary smoothness, and the fascination of their great size, with the two sets of cylinders and motion spinning like sewing machines, and their quietness in operation, are a supreme expression of the great but gentle power of steam which has opened up lines of communication all over the globe.

*One of a set of 25 Garratt engines
built by the
Beyer, Peacock Company
for the
New South Wales
Railway 1952*

Acknowledgement is due to the following for permission to reproduce illustrations:

JOHN ADAMS (COLOURVIEWS LTD) Curzon St, Birmingham opposite page 96; BIRMINGHAM CITY MUSEUM AND ART GALLERY page 82; BRITISH RAILWAYS BOARD chair page 84; CROWN COPYRIGHT, SCIENCE MUSEUM, LONDON page 17, *Catch me who Can* (model) page 19, pages 21, 24, 26 and 27, *Planet* page 39, pages 48 and 51, Liverpool and Manchester Rly coach (model) page 77, mechanism of Riggenbach locomotive page 101, mechanism of Snowdon locomotive page 102; ERIC DE MARE Euston arch page 99; GEORGE DOW page 35; P. C. GARRETT page 89; N. F. GURLEY Festiniog Rly page 105; C. HAMILTON ELLIS *Arundel* opposite page 72; JAPAN INFORMATION CENTRE page 53; JAPAN NATIONAL TOURIST ORGANISATION page 86; LAING ART GALLERY AND MUSEUM, NEWCASTLE UPON TYNE Newcastle Station (both views) opposite page 97; MUSEUM OF BRITISH TRANSPORT, CLAPHAM opening of Liverpool and Manchester Rly opposite page 17, Maidenhead and Britannia Bridges opposite page 32, Company arms and badges opposite pages 72 and 73, Queen Adelaide's coach page 77, parliamentary carriage page 79, Queen Victoria's day saloon opposite page 80, artist's impression of Queen Victoria's coach opposite page 81, page 81, Pullman interior 1876 page 84, page 87, Kings Cross Station opposite page 96; NATIONAL MONU-MENTS RECORD pages 92, 94 and 96, St Pancras exterior page 98, Euston interior page 99; RADIO TIMES HULTON PICTURE LIBRARY title page, Trevithick page 18, page 30, Chat Moss opposite page 33, Locke page 35, pages 37, 56/57, 65, 69, 75 and 100, Pilatus Rly page 102, Snowdon derailment page 103; SCIENCE MUSEUM, LONDON Stephen-son family (by courtesy) opposite page 16, Trevithick's London Railway page 18, Blenkinsop's locomotive page 19, page 23, page 25, page 31, page 33, page 34, page 36, *Patent* locomotive page 39, Kirtley's goods locomotive page 41, page 47, page 52, Liverpool and Manchester Rly train pages 78/79, St Pancras interior page 98, Pilatus Rly Railcar page 101, Fell locomotive page 105, page 106, page 108; ALLAN STEWART jacket and Vale of Rheidol train page 105; RICHARD TREVITHICK Trevithick's London carriage page 14; UNIVERSITY OF MANCHESTER INSTITUTE OF SCIENCE AND TECHNOLOGY pages 110/111; JOHN VAN RIEMSDIJK Stephenson's locomotive page 41, pages 43, 45, 49, 50 and 109; WALES TOURIST BOARD Snowdon train today page 103.

IAN ALLAN LTD diagrams from *Historic Railway Disasters* by O. S. Nock, pages 58, 61 and 64.